Coping with Bereavement from Death or Divorce

Coping with Bereavement from Death or Divorce

W. Keith Hafer, J.D., Ph.D.

PRENTICE-HALL, INC., Englewood Cliffs, New Jersey

*Coping with Bereavement from Death
or Divorce* by W. Keith Hafer, J.D., Ph.D.
Copyright © 1981 by W. Keith Hafer, J.D., Ph.D.

All rights reserved. No part of this book may be
reproduced in any form or by any means, except
for the inclusion of brief quotations in a review,
without permission in writing from the publisher.
Address inquiries to Prentice-Hall, Inc., Englewood
Cliffs, New Jersey 07632

Printed in the United States of America

Prentice-Hall International, Inc., London
Prentice-Hall of Australia, Pty. Ltd., Sydney
Prentice-Hall of Canada, Ltd., Toronto
Prentice-Hall of India Private Ltd., New Delhi
Prentice-Hall of Japan, Inc., Tokyo
Prentice-Hall of Southeast Asia Pte. Ltd., Singapore
Whitehall Books Limited, Wellington, New Zealand

10 9 8 7 6 5 4 3 2 1

Library of Congress Cataloging in Publication Data
Hafer, W. Keith.
Coping with bereavement from death or divorce.
Bibliography: p.
Includes index.
1. Loss (Psychology) 2. Bereavement—Psychological
aspects. 3. Death—Psychological aspects. 4. Divorce—
Psychological aspects. 5. Adjustment (Psychology)
I. Title.
BF575.D35H33   155.9'37   81-8679
                              AACR2

ISBN 0-13-172270-0
ISBN 0-13-172262-X (PBK)

This book is dedicated to the memory of Antoinette Thacker Hafer and to all men and women everywhere whose hearts have cried for a lost love or a broken dream. But most of all it is dedicated to their children, whose lives often are shattered and always changed by the permanent loss of a parent through death or divorce—for theirs is a very special need, one which plays a major role in the bereavement resulting from the changing structure of a family unit.

Acknowledgment

To my wife and counseling partner, Joyce Pennington Hafer, R.N., M.A., I wish to acknowledge my debt for her continual support in the preparation of this work, which has included the judgment flowing from her training and experience, and the wisdom flowing from her heart. Without her contribution my effort would have been much less effective than it may be; and my insights would have remained the unilateral and biased conclusions of the masculine mind, denied the balance of feminine understanding.

Introduction

Among the many ills to which man is heir, none is more excruciating than grief, and none is less revealed in science or philosophy.

The seven principal losses capable of producing stress in man are these:

- Loss of a loved one by death.
- Loss of a loved one by divorce.
- Loss of a treasured friendship.
- Loss of a country (or citizenship) by enemy or political action.
- Loss of a job or vocation.
- Loss of a home or business by economic disaster, fire, or other natural cause.
- Loss of capital that represents a substantial part of one's economic protection.

Each of these losses can produce grief; and when combined in any number, the effect can be a level of grief that is overpowering.

The basic purpose of this book, then, is to provide a review of the problems associated with the loss of a loved one through death or divorce, and to offer suggestions for coping with the various forms and manifestations of loss.

In addition, an effort has been made to provide insight into the dynamics of divorce, and to suggest techniques for preventing it. Where divorce already has occurred, the need and methods for attaining self-fulfillment are reviewed. And because single life is an avenue open to all divorced and widowed people, its pros and cons also are examined, along with the option of a relationship without marriage.

Finally, it is hoped that the insight about divorce and its far-reaching implications will provide an increased incentive to unhappy married couples to commit themselves to an examination in depth of their marriages and what divorce could mean to them and their children.

In the process of self-examination, it is hoped further that those for whom divorce seems to be the only practical solution can attain a new level of self-understanding. This should make it possible to survive divorce with an expanded self-identity and a new determination to use divorce as a growth experience, from which can come new strengths and an expanded life in the years that follow the ending of a marriage.

Contents

Introduction *vii*
1 The Pain of Loss 2
2 Loss by Death: How to Surmount It 10
3 The Trauma of a Broken Marriage: How to Survive It 28
4 Helping the Bereaved Child 46
5 Putting Your Life Back Together: Self-Determination After Bereavement 58
6 Can Divorce Be Avoided? 66
7 The Single Life: Its Joys and Sorrows 78
Bibliography 85
Index 93
About the Author 97

1
The Pain Of Loss

The Pain of Loss

In *Much Ado About Nothing,* William Shakespeare wrote "Everyman can handle grief but he that has it." And if it is *your* grief you are dealing with, you will be devastated beyond measure, bereft of all that has central meaning in your life, and deaf to the sinuous claims of all well-wishers that "it will pass."

Of course, the well-wishers are right. Your grief will, in time, abate. But the time of healing can be measured in years rather than months, and can be the most agonizing experience you will ever be forced to survive.

The purpose of this book is to make your time of grieving shorter and your return to a balanced life quicker. In the process of offering aids to healing, it also can provide important insights to help you in your knowledge of the dynamics of grief—for if you are able to understand not only what is happening to you, but *why* it is happening, and that it happens to all who are bereaved, you will be better able to deal with the pain of grief and overcome it.

In writing about the loss of a love object which produces grief, it should be stated in the beginning that extensive field research by the author—as well as a careful review of the professional literature concerning the bereavements of death and divorce—indicates that there is little discernable difference in the potential symptoms, depth, or duration of grief which each form of loss can bring. In addition, the actual quality and extent of the grief that accompanies the loss of a mate by physical death, as well as from the death of a marriage, inevitably is responsive to the same seven factors listed later in this chapter.

For this reason, although the grief of death, as separate from the grief of divorce, will be dealt with in different chapters—in the hope that this separation will be useful to those readers who suffer from only one form of these two bereavements—you will find occasional cross-references, which result from the commonality of symptoms of each form of loss.

Because of the psychological trauma associated with the

The Pain of Loss

loss of a love object, grief can be classified as a mental illness. It also can be potentially disturbing to physical functions to a degree which can be as disabling as a serious physical injury. To better understand grief, it may help to perceive it as a reactive depression, or separation anxiety, which is *part of a process,* rather than a state. And assuming that the loss of a partner by death or divorce is not desired, the process of grieving usually will follow this chronological path:

Denial of loss ("He can't be gone!")
Realization of loss ("Oh, God, it's true. He's gone forever!")
Feeling of abandonment, alarm, and anxiety. ("Dear God, how will I ever make it alone?")
Despair, crying, physical numbness, mental confusion, indecisiveness
Restlessness (a product of anxiety), insomnia, loss of appetite, irritability, loss of self-control, wandering mind
Pining (the physical pain and agony of grieving) and a search for some token remembrance of the lost love object
Anger ("Why did he have to die?; Why didn't he take better care of himself?; I gave him the best years of my life! Now what do I do?")
Guilt ("I should have taken better care of him. It's my fault he got sick!")
Feelings of loss of self, or total emptiness. ("Half of me is gone forever!")
Longing (the dull ache that won't go away, even when with others)
Identification with your lost partner by assuming some of his traits, attitudes, or mannerisms
Profound depression ("I just want to die!")
Pathological aspects, such as a myriad of minor aches and ailments, and a marked tendency toward hypochondria. ("Who will take care of me now?")
Voluntary return to society

The Pain of Loss

The diminishment of grief symptoms, and the beginning of full recovery

HOW LONG DOES GRIEVING LAST?

The answer to this question depends on many factors, the principal ones being these:

1. The degree of attachment or love for your lost partner.
2. The period of psychological preparation for your loss, if any.
3. Your age and general health at the time of bereavement.
4. Your financial security when bereavement occurs.
5. Your vocational commitment at the time of bereavement.
6. The extent of your supportive family network.
7. The presence and affection of a close circle of friends to help you cope.

Grief begins at the time of loss and builds slowly as recognition of loss assumes reality. In extreme cases, shallow grief can be dissipated in a period of weeks, while deep grief can remain for an unnumbered period of years. Two examples from the author's files: a widow who did her husband's every bidding, subordinating her life to his for forty years, on his death heaved a sigh of relief and began for the first time to live for herself, honoring and loving her husband's memory, but savoring to the fullest her newly found freedom; and a man who lost his wife to his next-door neighbor, and retained every symptom of deep bereavement twenty-seven years later.

THE PHYSICAL ASPECTS OF GRIEF

Like the emotional pain of loss, the physical manifestations can take a myriad of forms. However, most research shows seven

The Pain of Loss

symptoms to be most common among people in a state of bereavement, as follows:

1. Waves of physical distress marked by crying, sobbing, and sometimes by screaming.
2. Closing up of the throat muscles, making swallowing uncomfortable.
3. A feeling of choking and loss of breath.
4. Heavy and repeated sighing.
5. An empty feeling in the abdomen.
6. Lack of muscle power; muscle aches and pains.
7. A feeling of extreme tension, as if you're going to explode inside.

Like the duration of grief, its physical manifestations are responsive to the same seven factors that modify its term.

GRIEF IN MEN VERSUS WOMEN

Although loss is equally painful for both sexes, there are these notable differences in bereavement felt by men and by women:

In both death and divorce, men speak of having lost a part of themselves. Women feel they have been deserted.

Women find work an antidote to sorrow. More sustained in their work drive by their wives, men who suddenly are alone in life experience a noticeable diminishment in their ability to concentrate on their work.

Tending to be more realistic than women, men generally have more self-control in bereavement.

Perhaps because of the frequent disparity between men and

The Pain of Loss

women in commitment to a partnership, men tend to have more guilt feelings about death or divorce, but lose them sooner.

Men have less personal concern than women about mental breakdowns caused by grief.

In loss by death, men are less disturbed by funerals than women, and are more critical of undertakers and funeral expenses.

In loss by divorce or death, men have less concern about finances (as they generally have more control over them).

In divorce bereavement, men who do not receive custody of children tend to grieve longer than women and to experience a deeper sense of loss.

In loss by death, men are prone to recover emotionally sooner than women.

When a partnership ends by death or divorce, men generally remarry sooner than women.

Men miss the sexual side of marriage more than women, and usually are quicker to replace it in their lives.

Men are less fatalistic about loss, and less prone to blame themselves.

No matter what the dynamics of the loss of a partner, it can be the most shattering event you ever will experience. And because death is the ultimate end of living, and divorce now occurs in more than four marriages out of ten, the potential loss of a partner should be faced by all who give their hearts to another.

The Pain of Loss

Concerning death, man has yet to find a way to avoid the ultimate deterioration of the body. For this reason, psychological preparation for death should begin in childhood. If one believes in the immortality of the soul, an acceptance of death as the doorway to a new and fuller life can be a source of supreme comfort. And if one believes that there is no life after death, it can be viewed as a welcome surcease at last from the pain of living. Regardless of one's view concerning death, a useful goal of society well could be the open recognition of the inevitability that our life form must one day end, and a willingness to share death as an experience common to us all. From such sharing could come new strengths for man to pay death's debt without demur.

2

Loss By Death

How to Surmount It

Loss by Death: How to Surmount It

The statistics of widowhood are shocking. Today there are 10 million widows in the United States, with 700,000 more joining their ranks each year. Of this number only 16,000 will find another husband in any one year, with the chances of remarriage decreasing as the age of the widow increases.

The unpleasant odds are that three out of every four wives will be widowed, with their loss occurring between the ages of fifty and sixty. Most of these widows will suffer a level of bereavement that will vary from painful to acute, and which will last from twelve to twenty-four months or longer, depending on the depth of emotional attachment the widow had to her husband, and the length of time involved in the forewarning of death—the longer the warning, the less acute the bereavement is likely to be.

Because of the large number of women who already are widows, and the even greater number who one day will be faced with widowhood, it is hoped that this chapter will provide insights to help alleviate the stress of past, present, and future widows.

The word *widow* means empty in Sanskrit, and it best describes the physical state of most women who have lost their mates. This feeling of emptiness must be filled before recovery from your loss can take place. And as it can only be filled with human contact, it is important to know what social support you can expect to receive in your state of grief.

As a widow, you can be sure of receiving certain preferred treatment by society in general. And although this treatment may not be supportive enough to counterbalance your grief, it *will* be important to you in your recovery from bereavement.

First, you will receive the full respect and moral support of your social group and of society in general, and you will find friends and strangers alike eager to touch your hand in comfort and encouragement. Prominent among your comforters will be

Loss by Death: How to Surmount It

family members, neighbors, members of your church (if you habitually devote the Sabbath morning to formal spiritual worship), and the clergyman who leads you in your search for God. You also will be accorded the respectful attention and good wishes of all members of your community with whom you come in periodic contact; you will receive their tender expressions of sorrow and vague offers of help "of any kind." And all of this helps with the *social* aspects of your grief, reinforcing your knowledge that society in general approves of your blameless state of widowhood.

Value of a different kind will accrue to you as a widow from the attitudes of special courts that have been designed for the express purpose of protecting widows and their issue from those who would prey on them in their extremity. This too is comforting, and provides valuable support.

In exchange for the unrestrained approval of society and the church, and the assiduous protection of the courts, you will be expected to conform to certain standards of conduct which are rooted in ancient social custom, and which today can be onerous and restrictive.

Among the public acts expected of you as a widow will be some sort of ceremonial leave-taking of your husband, such as the ordering of a funeral or commemorative cremation service, the acceptance of flowers or other gifts in tribute to his memory, and the arranging of a brief but suitable eulogy to sum up the public virtues of your late mate. In some communities and in some cultures you also will be expected to wear black or dark clothing for a suitable period of time, and to observe sober and decorous conduct in public places.

When the period following death—which has just been described—is ended, and you have made obeisance to all of the social requirements, *what comes next?* What are the pitfalls of your new widowhood, and how can you avoid them?

To help you recognize and deal with the principal

Loss by Death: How to Surmount It

problems you can expect to encounter as a widow, they are reviewed below by type.

SOCIAL TRIALS FOR WIDOWS

Right after your husband died, all your friends rallied around, giving you support without limit. And although you were too stunned by sorrow to fully appreciate their condolences and solicitude, the general idea broke through your grief that the world that had been your social microcosm was solidly behind you; and you derived great comfort from the knowledge that nothing had changed except the death of your mate. Don't you believe it! *Everything* has changed, as you will learn.

First off, you will find that our society is inflexibly geared to the dyadic approach, or pairing. If your children are grown and leading separate lives, or if you have no children, there is no natural place for you in the social structure; the regular social invitations you exchanged with other couples will slowly dwindle down, then quietly disappear.

This is not to say that you will be socially ostracized. Far from it. If you are a churchgoer you will find your Sunday greetings as warm as ever, and your departure from old friends and acquaintances equally effusive, with smiling requests such as "Let's get together soon, dear!" But "soon" has a way of never coming.

Barely before your partner's remains have found their last resting place you will be inundated with offers of "help" from the husbands of your women friends and neighbors. Slipping quietly into your kitchen, they will say variations of this: "Call on me, my dear, for anything you need. Absolutely *anything*. I admired your husband a lot, and although I know I can't fill his shoes, just know that I'm available at any time!"

Loss by Death: How to Surmount It

Of course there *are* friends and neighbors who are concerned with your leaking kitchen sink, or the loose board in your front steps, or the peeling paint on the north side of your house, and they truly are the salt of the earth. Unfortunately, there is a serious shortage of this kind of salt, and the probable message sent by your friendly male neighbor was this: "I know you're going to miss sex with your husband, and I'd be happy to meet your need in a perfectly discreet way, of course, seeing as how we're such close neighbors and all."

For some widows sex was a trial, to be borne with fortitude and grace. For others it was a joy, reaffirming the heart's choice with each encounter. If you happen to be one of the stoical few, your husband's death worked no hardship on you. However, if yours was a vibrant physical union, you will in time begin to long for the passionate touch of your erstwhile lover, and your cross of loneliness will take on a new dimension. In search of relief from the absence of eros in your life, your choices as a widow are few, and clearly circumscribed. First, you can of course accept the kindly offers of your neighbors' husbands, and begin to live a life of dangerous adultery.

If this social aberration is repellent to you, you may choose to become a predator yourself, joining mature social clubs (especially dancing groups) in the hope of finding an unattached male of suitable age and disposition to become your periodic lover. If this becomes your choice, you may find a solution to your problem that meets your physical needs without requiring a commitment you may not be ready or eager to make; this is the path chosen by many modern women of strong sexual appetites. At worst, you may be talked about by jealous friends and acquaintances (who lack your drive and your honesty). At best, your sexual encounter, if entered into with discretion as well as passion, may lead to a lasting liaison, which you may wish to make permanent or sanctify by clergy.

Loss by Death: How to Surmount It

FINANCIAL PITFALLS FOR WIDOWS

Although the law is zealous in its aim to protect the surviving spouse, the world is filled with fast operators who are ready and eager to accept the challenge of separating widows from their dowers as quickly and painlessly as possible.

Unfortunately, many of these sharpshooters have taken on the coloration of credibility; their fleecing techniques are legitimate in all but purpose. When faced with an introduction to such a person, you often will confuse him with an attorney or a banker—for his disguise is the very naturalness of his demeanor, and his offers to help you with your investments (sale of your house, consolidation of your real estate, etc.) are highly legitimate, and often follow the recommendation of a third party whom you know and have no reason to distrust.

Unless your husband was a lawyer or banker or accountant who appointed a trusted professional associate to administer his will and oversee his estate, your best bet is to seek an appointment with a senior officer of your bank and ask him to recommend a successful, ethical, and competent lawyer to whom you can turn for honest and knowledgeable guidance in rebuilding the financial structure of your newly single life.

If your husband had an account with a stock brokerage firm, you will receive an early call from his customers' representative. When he or she calls, take careful note of his or her advice, and ask for a written summary of your husband's account along with a recommendation for its future course. When it is received, take it to your lawyer for review. In the end, you will have to decide whether you want or need high-return, short-run investments, or those of lower, fixed yield and longer term. You also may have to decide between the risk of stocks over the (relative) security of bonds. But whatever your decision, be alert to any effort to switch your investments from one source to another at

Loss by Death: How to Surmount It

frequent intervals. This technique is called "churning", and is a devious device to generate the maximum amount of sales commission by the multiple turning over of your investments.

Unless your husband was an insurance company executive, or sales representative, the world of insurance may be a mystery to you; and you will do well to seek highly ethical insurance counsel (recommended by your lawyer) before you give serious consideration to any insurance program proposed for your protection. This particularly includes *all* forms of health and disaster (cancer) insurance, many of which are offered by companies marginally operating within the law.

If you have inherited real estate, either improved or unimproved, you are fair game for all real estate agents who seek to list your property for sale. To protect yourself, identify and personally call on the president of the local board of realtors, and ask him or her to guide you in any real estate transactions that may result from your new status as a widow.

When he or she has collected all relevant facts and carefully analyzed your real estate equities, ask for a summary of your position, along with recommendations for your best plan of action.

If you know any officer of a savings and loan association, your next visit should be to his or her office. If you have no such acquaintance, ask an officer of your bank to recommend such a person, and make an appointment to see him or her. In the ensuing meeting, show your realtor's plan to the savings and loan officer, and ask the officer's judgment. If it is markedly different from the advice your realtor has offered, seek a third opinion from your lawyer. And then make up your own mind, using the best judgment you can muster to deal with the facts at hand.

If you and your husband have been home owners, and if your children are grown and living under their own roofs, you will

Loss by Death: How to Surmount It

receive much advice from well-meaning friends and business counselors to consider selling your home and moving to a "carefree" condominium of smaller size. If your home is mortgage free, one of the arguments advanced for this move will be the opportunity to pay less for a condominium than you will realize from the sale of your house; it will be pointed out that you can invest the difference in income-producing equities.

Although such advice is sound enough in theory, whether or not it is appropriate for you is a question you should carefully explore. Even if you find the arithmetic attractive, and are able to locate a condominium that seems to meet your every need, proceed with excessive care. For not only are all condominiums not good and/or safe long-term investments—regardless of compelling arithmetic—they seldom are built to afford the level of auditory privacy you have come to expect as a home owner, and you may well find your neighbors' stomach problems less than confidential if their bathrooms happen to be on the opposite side of your walls. Worse than this, unless your building has individual air conditioning and heating units that are properly designed and insulated for quiet operation, you also may find the central duct system an interesting and indiscriminate carrier of private conversations and personal acts.

And perhaps the most offensive of all trials is the possibility that your apartment ceiling may be under the roof where the central air-conditioning system is located. If such should be the case, your life in warm weather will resemble a work shift in a boiler factory, as the condenser(s) switch on and off endlessly.

And if this were not enough to deter you, consider with care two more building features: the floors and the windows. If the building is older, and was built with living comfort rather than quick profit in mind, your floors well may be finished with tile, terrazzo, or parquet—all of which are beautiful to the eye and desirable in the extreme. However, they also are active sound conductors, and if your neighbor in the apartment above

Loss by Death: How to Surmount It

you uses area rugs, you will hear every tap of every heel, night and day, over your head.

As for the windows, most modern architects seem to have forgotten that their main purpose was to provide easy passage of cross-ventilated air throughout the living space of each room. As a result, many modern condominiums feature a combination of a few horizontally sliding windows, wall-to-wall sliding doors onto a balcony or terrace, and *no other device* for the passage of air except the ubiquitous and ever noisy air-conditioning equipment.

Even if you can afford the monthly maintenance fee for your condominium—a not inconsiderable sum in many cases—and believe that all of your physical needs for a quiet and comfortable life are met in the condominium of your choice, consider with care the psychological needs that were satisfied so often by digging in your garden, planting your favorite flowers, or just watching the birds wheel and land in your trees, calling their seasonal greetings to each other and to you. Sometimes, for some people, *this* aspect of home ownership more than outweighs any possible convenience or economic advantage of apartment living, but you and you alone must be the final judge.

Hopefully, you are in a group of widows whose annual incomes from all sources total ten thousand dollars or more. If so, you are likely to find one or more of the above suggestions to be of practical value. However, if you happen to be one of the 40 percent who live below the so-called poverty level, other suggestions can be helpful to you, as follows:

> Check your eligibility for Social Security benefits under your husband's coverage, as well as for Medicare and Medicaid, all part of the federal Old Age Assistance Act, to which every citizen has some form of entitlement.

Check your eligibility for food stamps. This form of federal support is not a charity, but a part of a program of social welfare supported by the taxes your husband paid over the years; it is a vested right for all who meet the eligibility requirements.

If you live in the last home you shared with your husband, and for personal reasons wish to continue to enjoy this form of housing independence, consider sharing your home with a single and compatible relative or friend, to whom the joys of life in a single-family dwelling might have appeal. Such a solution, when entered into with care and mutual accord, can become one of the most satisfactory and supportive living arrangements you can make; it often results in a new level of contentment and companionship, as well as in better health and longer life.

Many communities, particularly in the Southeast and Southwest, which attract retirees and sun worshipers to warmer climates, have developed elaborate social support systems for widows and widowers, as well as older citizens. However, no matter where you live, be sure to check with your local United Fund office and city hall for a list of facilities that may be available at very low cost or no cost at all. Such services often include those that appear in alphabetical order at the end of this chapter.

So far we have dealt largely with the practical side of survival. Now that it is out of the way, the even more important aspect of your inner or psychological life must be examined and reinforced.

If you are a widow who has had the time or inclination to recognize the fact that most women today outlive their husbands, the chances are high that you will experience a much shorter period of mourning, for the reason that your psyche has been preparing you for an ultimate separation in a way which not only anticipates (and thereby dilutes) grief, but which actually can serve to endow the joy of living with one's mate with a deeper and richer meaning.

However, if you are an average widow who has assiduously avoided thought or conversation about the potential death of your mate, you can expect to share the principal stresses of your new state, which include those appearing below.

PRINCIPAL STRESSES OF WIDOWHOOD

Loss of social identity as a wife, and acceptance of a lower social identity as a widow. If you are one who had primarily identified yourself with a husband and children, your sense of loss will include your personal identity.

A general sense of confusion, which will be expressed in memory lapses, difficulty in concentrating, and wandering thoughts.

Fear about financial security. Although many widows are well off financially, the majority find themselves with a reduced income, which can be a source of constant stress.

Intense and pervasive loneliness. If your union was one of extreme rapport, you will be lonely for the *person* of your husband. If it was less than idyllic, you will be lonely for a *partner*.

Depression usually is a companion of loneliness. If you experience depression, it can produce these symptoms, in varying and fluctuating degrees:

Loss by Death: How to Surmount It

> A feeling of hopelessness and despair.
>
> Changes in level of physical activity.
>
> Loss of self-esteem and feeling of self-worth.
>
> Fear of rejection, which may cause social withdrawal.
>
> Inordinate sensitivity to the words or actions of others.
>
> Unexplained irritability.
>
> Free-floating and often withheld anger.
>
> Feelings of guilt and self-blame.
>
> Extreme dependency on others.
>
> Suicidal feelings or acts.

All of these stresses will be disruptive of your well-being, and as death is the most traumatic of all life changes, a high level of stress—or a combination of many stresses—can result in physical illness, the body's response to shock and its effort to immobilize you while healing takes place.

However, of all the stresses you may experience, none can be more devastating than depression. The following suggestions are offered for coping with the depression that can follow the loss of a loved one:

Accept your grief and express it. If you feel like crying, cry. It is nature's way of reducing stress. And take time to grieve, for grieving is a vital process in healing.

If possible, share your feelings with someone you trust. This will

Loss by Death: How to Surmount It

help restore your perspective and reduce your feeling of being alone.

Change your daily routine. This will be of value in freeing up your frozen tensions. If financially possible for you, take a vacation (if you are employed), or a trip (if you don't work). If no one you care for is available to go with you, go alone. Change is healing. And if you are truly open to new friendships, they are sure to follow.

Engage in some form of physical activity appropriate to your age, such as tennis, swimming, dancing, bicycling, jogging, or just plain walking. And try to do it daily. If none of these activities appeal to you, or are not possible for some reason, join a class in Yoga. Not only will it help to tone up your body and work off tensions, but it can soothe your battered spirit. It also can lead to new friendships, which you need to form.

Try to find something you can do well, and do it often. This will help rebuild your impaired self-esteem.

Focus your energy on someone else—perhaps someone who is old or sick or lonely. This will help take your mind off your loss, and will aid you in conquering self-pity.

Take a good, honest look at your appearance, decide how it might be improved, and set about changing it for the better. This will improve your self-image.

Get involved in activities with others—anything that takes you out of the house and broadens your horizons and your social contacts. And be open to sharing yourself and your identity with new acquaintances. This will encourage them to share in return, and will plant the seeds of friendship.

Loss by Death: How to Surmount It

If you have any latent skill or unused training, consider putting it to use vocationally, either full or part time. This will help to rebuild your feeling of independence. It also will augment your income and help reduce any financial pressure you may be feeling.

If you have no discernible or marketable skills, and married too young to have acquired any significant training, consider returning to school—about which there is more later, in Chapter 5.

If there are valid reasons why a return to the marketplace or to school is not practical for you—such as physical infirmity or advanced age—consider pooling your resources with those of another person in similar financial circumstances. This should be a person you like, respect, and feel comfortable with, but it can be male or female—the U.S. Census Bureau reports a total of 1.1 million couples known to be living together without benefit of clergy, many of them attaining a higher and more comfortable standard of living by joining the purchasing power of two incomes.

If your depression persists and/or leads you to serious thoughts of self-destruction, seek professional help. This usually can be found in your local community at one or more of the social service agencies that receive their support from public funds. Prominent among such groups are family service agencies and mental health clinics.

If you have a deep religious orientation, turn to your church and draw on the spiritual meaning it has for you. If you are one who has an unexpressed sense of identity with an infinite Father or Supreme Being, devote twenty minutes before breakfast each morning to a time of quiet prayer and meditation, in which you seek to become one with your own inner or Christ self. Like nothing else, this exercise in opening yourself to the healing

Loss by Death: How to Surmount It

powers of the spirit within can restore you to new and exuberant mental and physical health, and can help to direct you toward your own greatest fulfillment in the years ahead. At the same time, this sense of unity with the spark of God within—sought and found in daily meditation—can restore you to a feeling of being together with a permanent and highly personal source of comfort, and can take the bitter edge off your desperate feeling of being alone.

It also can endow you with an aura of peace, which will attract to you others whose heavy inner burdens also are being carried alone, thus bringing to you new opportunities for the deep friendship that can flow from common needs and shared experiences of the spirit.

As stated earlier, depression and loneliness usually are companion symptoms in bereavement. Like depression, loneliness can lead to excessive suffering, and can destroy your ability to function in a rational way. Because loneliness is an emotional response common to the bereavements of divorce as well as death, it is covered in some detail in the following chapter; the suggestions offered there for coping with loneliness will be of benefit to all widows (and widowers) who are experiencing this strong and potentially crippling emotion.

Probably because widowers as a group usually have been more dependent on marriage for personal satisfaction than their wives, and usually experience greater difficulty in coping successfully with household management, 50 percent of all widowers will remarry within the first year; most will enter into subsequent legal unions much sooner than widows. Also, although many of us tend to repeat our mistakes, the second marriage experience for most widowers will be a positive one, benefiting from lessons learned in the first marriage.

Nonetheless, most widowers will experience the same manifestations, if not the same level of bereavement as widows;

Loss by Death: How to Surmount It

and men who have lost their wives through death may find the suggestions made to widows in this chapter to be of value.

TYPICAL SOCIAL SERVICES OF POSSIBLE VALUE TO WIDOWS
(Available in many cities)

Adult activity groups
Aging advocacy groups
Blind/visually handicapped services
Credit and budget counseling
Crisis intervention center
Community human relations services
Community recreation/culture activities
Deaf services
Dental care services
Drug counseling services
Emergency alcohol abuse services
Employment assistance for low-income persons
Employment assistance for physically handicapped
Employment assistance for senior citizens
Extension education opportunities
Eyeglass provision
Financial assistance during employment training
General emergency financial assistance
General medical care
General medical diagnostic services
Glaucoma prevention and detection
Health counseling information
Hearing testing and evaluating
Home health care services
Job placement and referral
Job training
Landlord and tenant rights

Loss by Death: How to Surmount It

Legal assistance center
Meals on Wheels, for shut-ins
Neighborly Centers (where one free hot meal is served each day in a social atmosphere at a church parish house, to which those without cars are transported in free buses)
Recreation activities for the handicapped
Unemployment compensation
Veterans' benefits for dependents

3
The Trauma of a Broken Marriage

How to Survive It

The Trauma of a Broken Marriage: How to Survive It

If your form of loss has been the death of a marriage, you can be feeling any or all of the symptoms of the bereavement of physical death; and this chapter is written for you.

First, if you happen to have any ethical or religious proscriptions concerning the sanctity and eternal nature of marriage vows, or if you are feeling shameful and socially outcast because your union was severed long before death did you part, perhaps you'll feel better—or at least less like a pariah—if you take a look at the astonishing statistics about divorce which follow:

In 1860 the divorce rate in the United States was .3 per 100. By 1980 it had climbed to 44 divorces for every 100 marriages.

As of 1978, 16 million Americans had been divorced at some point in their lives; one million divorces are now being filed each year, and the astonishing projection is made for 10 million divorces each year in the USA by 1986.

In addition to the number of divorce actions now filed yearly, it is estimated that at least one million more couples will resort to separation or desertion, and that an additional one million couples will continue to live under the same roof, but be psychologically divorced.

Second only to Sweden in the number of divorces, the United States today accords a degree of public acceptance of divorce never dreamed of only a few years ago. Proof of this remarkable change in our social mores is found in the large number of divorced people who occupy important and highly visible positions. Notable among them are a U.S. President, the wife of a former U.S. President, a former U.S. Vice-President and his wife, U.S. Supreme Court justices (one of whom was multiply married while on the bench), governors of states, U.S. senators and representatives, university presidents, and a growing number of clergymen.

In short, by the ninth decade of the twentieth century, divorce in our land has become epidemic. Your problems as a divorced person are shared by people everywhere, at all socioeconomic levels, and in all vocations and professions.

THE SYMPTOMS OF DIVORCE BEREAVEMENT

As stated in the first chapter, the loss of a partner by divorce can produce any or all of the same symptoms—and to the same depth and for an equal duration—as a loss by death.

The reasons for this are obvious: Divorce, like death, results in an extensive reorganization of one's life, life-style, and economics; it nearly always has a profound impact on one's own self-concept and relationship with others. In addition, if there are children, divorce changes the course of life for an entire family unit.

In 1979 an American physician named R. H. Rahe revealed the results of a detailed study of crises that occur in the lives of most of us at one time or another. In so doing, Dr. Rahe developed a scale of intensity of stress resulting from the most common life events, which revealed that people rate intensity of stress on a scale of 1 to 100 as follows:

Death of a spouse	100
Divorce	73
Marital separation	65

In short, the pain associated with the loss of a partner by any means is one of the most stressful events you can ever experience. And although there is no way you can avoid this stress, it may be of value to review for you the symptoms most frequently encountered among divorced people. Thus, for whatever psychological value it may have for you, you will know that your suffering is a common agony experienced by most others who are divorced, in the following order:

Anxiety/Fear

Sadness/Regret

Anger/Frustration

Insecurity

Loneliness

Guilt

Longing

In addition to these most common symptoms of divorce, others frequently reported are found in the following statements of recently divorced people:

"I'm shaky, scared, afraid of the dark."

"I have violent mood swings."

"I have lots of colds, sore throats, and other minor ailments I never had before."

"I feel disconnected."

"I miss the predictability, the continuity of marriage."

"There's a void in my life, an emptiness, where my mate's imprint once was."

The Trauma of a Broken Marriage: How to Survive It

"There's an ache that won't go away."

"I can't sleep; I need someone to share my life!"

"I feel so alone."

"I feel rejected, unwanted, and lost."

"God, how I dread holidays, any holiday, especially Christmas!"

"I need to be needed again."

If the pain reported by others is the pain you are feeling, know that there is hope. For although you can never forget the high moments of joy you shared with your mate, and the exhilaration of being part of a whole social unit, time is nature's greatest healer; in time, your pain will abate and your anguish fade. Until that time has come for you, however, there are supports you can turn to, aids you can use to relieve your stress. They are dealt with below.

First we will take a look at *anxiety* and *fear*. Opposite sides of the same coin, both are responses to things over which you have limited or no control—a characteristic of divorce. For even in an amicable ending of a marriage, you are setting forth on uncharted seas, and all things unknown hold within them the threat of disaster. When we can clearly see the future—no matter how black it may be—we are able to prepare psychologically to meet it. But when the future is obscured from us, we are inclined to invest it with unnamed threats and perils; this is especially true when our defenses are down and we are drained of our reserve emotional strength. Therefore, the best and quickest way to combat your anxiety or fear is to bring it out into the open and try to analyze it. To help you do this, please turn to the end of this chapter and fill in your answers on the Fear

The Trauma of a Broken Marriage: How to Survive It

Questionnaire. When you have finished, study your answers to see if they have given you any insight about this emotion as it affects you. Then turn back to the text and continue reading.

There is no way to predict what responses you have made to these five questions, but there is one certainty about your answers: They have helped you to identify your fears and to determine whether they are physical or emotional, real or imagined. And they have helped you to face what it is you fear. Once faced, fear will not necessarily disappear, but it will lose some of its power to immobilize you. You can then begin the necessary task of learning to live with and accept your fears for what they are, while doing everything in your power to remove their cause.

Now, let's take a closer look at *sadness* and *regret*. If you are experiencing either of these feelings, the chances are high that you were not the moving party in your divorce action, and that it came as a shock to you. Where such is the case, there has been time for your partner to adjust to a loss which he or she was planning to bring about. Even though the instigators of divorce often feel the symptoms of bereavement, the depth and duration of their symptoms generally are less severe, for they were able to begin earlier the psychological process of withdrawal from a marriage which must precede any recovery from the feeling of loss.

Therefore, your own first task in coping with sadness and regret is this: Face the fact that your marriage has ended, and build from there. Until you are able to do this, it's all uphill. But once faced, acknowledged, and accepted for what it is—a broken life—the worst is over; and the healing process can begin.

In taking this first and perhaps most terrifying step toward your psychological recovery, you have removed its greatest power to hurt you. You have brought yourself to a point of objectivity from which you can begin to release the pain and sorrow related to a past that, for you, must be forever ended.

In the process of letting go of this sorrow and regret, you will find the need to cry, perhaps to scream and beat your hands against the wall. Follow this impulse whenever it appears, for crying is nature's way of cleansing and healing. If you have friends who are prone to say "Don't cry; it'll be OK," don't heed their well-meaning counsel—for it will not, it can never be OK for you until you are able to cry as often and as much as your heart needs.

And now we come to *anger* and *frustration*. Perhaps you are experiencing neither one of these feelings. If so, you are one of the lucky (or sainted) ones, in whose heart anger never grows. But if you are like most of us, you are feeling angry and hurt, and your level of frustration is nearly boundless—for you gave your life into the keeping of another, and your trust has been betrayed.

In overcoming anger, you are truly cleansing your soul, for anger is a spirit poison that can lead to devastating physical manifestations; there has been at least one well-trained and long-experienced psychiatrist who has seen in anger and frustration the seeds of cancer. Thus, your need to break the bonds of anger could not be greater.

In your effort to accomplish this difficult task, you will be required to face the anger of bereavement for what it is: the dark side of your own ego—for it is the impairment of your self-image that is involved with anger. What your mind is really telling you here is not so much that you hurt as that you have been deserted and left alone, to live or die in your own despair.

So again, as in coping with sadness, in dealing with your anger you will be required to face the fact of your rejection. If you are wiser and stronger than most, you will be concerned not only with losing anger, but with understanding the causal factors involved in your rejection. By this understanding, you will acquire the strength and purpose to bring about modifications in those personality factors that led to your desertion. In this way alone you can at last assure yourself of a happiness to come of which you were not before capable.

If the strength required to accomplish such a metamorphosis is not yours to command, your insight into the real cause of your anger can in time help it to dissolve, and can pave the way to a renewed self-image with which you can live in harmony and peace.

As for the *insecurity* you may be feeling, if its level is high, the chances are that it reflects the change in your financial situation which divorce has brought about. If this is the case, you will be required to accept your circumstances as they are now, while you work in all ways possible to improve your condition. In the process of coping with your feelings of financial (and physical) insecurity, it will be helpful to accept the fact as it is: Your life has changed in every aspect. And although such acceptance will not of itself increase your security, it will release for your use the psychic energy you will need to rebuild your life in ways that provide the protection you require.

In working toward this goal, it is important that you understand the psychological dynamics involved. Before, the fact and feeling of your security was drawn from your dependence on another; now it rests largely upon you and you alone. The only answer to your heart's question, "Can I make it on my own?" must be a resounding "Yes, I can!"

A distillation of thousands of years of philosophy concerned with positive thinking shows us that anything man can imagine, he can bring to be. We have abundant proof of this in space capsules that transport men to and return them from other planets, in microsurgery, and in the economic and political recovery from total chaos of countries vanquished in armed conflict a few short years ago. Therefore, know in your heart that whatever level of security you wish to attain—without limitation—can and will be yours if you can determine what

The Trauma of a Broken Marriage: How to Survive It

goals you wish to strive for, and fix them clearly in your mind as being capable of attainment in the short, intermediate, or long term.

The very process of choosing your goals and setting them to timetables, designed to bring you security in a series of progressions, is the first and most important step. Take it, and you are on your way to building a life based on your own strengths, which may bend but never bow to the slings and arrows of outrageous fortune, no matter how painful they may once more become.

Of all the agonies of bereavement, none is more pervasive than *loneliness*. It is the fear of being alone that drives many to marry unwisely and in haste; and, having done so, it is this same fear that holds many unhappy marriages together in a life of mutual neurotic dependency on the physical presence of each other.

Thus, when the physical separation of divorce comes to those who were victims of the fear of loneliness, it can be devastating beyond measure, and it can destroy life. Therefore, if loneliness is one of the crosses you bear, take comfort in the knowledge that there are social techniques to combat it, and psychological disciplines which can help you to overcome it.

But first let's examine for a moment such a small but painful fear as being afraid of the dark, which so many bereaved people experience. This particular fear is always with us, waiting to be released by its sister fear of being alone—for fear of darkness is man's inheritance from simian ancestors (if you believe in evolution), or from our soul memory of the darkness that opposes light (if you believe in the divine creation of man and the constant challenge by the forces of evil, or darkness). If this particular fear is a part of your loneliness, accept it as a natural manifestation, and combat it in the only practical way: Keep a light or lights burning at night in places where fear, for you, lurks most ominously.

On the social side, the first canon in overcoming loneliness is this: Make friends—for they are the only fabric in which loneliness can be smothered. To make a friend, it is first necessary that you be open to friendship, willing and eager to give something of yourself in the process. It is only through this giving that true friendship, the supportive level of friendship that you need, can grow.

To make friends it is, of course, necessary that you go where people are. It also is necessary that you select those places where people with whom you have the greatest compatibility can be found. If your interest lies in sports or body culture or physical control, a neighborhood or civic tennis court or swimming pool or a Yoga class can be a good place to start.

If dancing turns you on, most communities offer some facility where single dancers can meet others who seek dancing partners. If this is not true where you live, perhaps a community college offers classes in ballroom, square, or western dancing; and this is a good first option. If you happen to have adequate means, or are willing to make an investment disproportionate to the size of your purse, there are private dancing schools where you are sure to meet other lonely people whose needs and interests are similar to your own.

If you have a good singing voice, or even experience joy in singing off-key, nearly every church of any size will welcome you to its choir. The time of practice with other members can open new social horizons for you, as well as occupy your lonely hours.

If none of these activities appeal to you, or if there is some reason why they are not possible for you, many churches in all communities have singles' groups which meet periodically. There you can enjoy the fellowship of socializing which must precede any relationship that can be of real consequence to you.

If you happen to be a divorced person with young children who make it difficult for you to seek social avenues of friendship, contact the Parents Without Partners group in your community. There you are sure to find others who share one or more of the problems of living alone that plague you, including loneliness.

In addition to these suggestions for overcoming loneliness by exposing yourself to social contacts with other people who may be alone, you very likely can supply ideas of your own which will bring you in touch with social groups related to your interests.

Among the psychological aids that can be of value in combating loneliness is a thoughtful assessment of your own feelings about this emotion. You can make this assessment by answering the few questions about yourself that appear at the end of this chapter in the Loneliness Questionnaire. As in the use of the Fear Questionnaire, please fill in your answers with care, then study them to see what insights you may have derived from this exercise. After you have considered your answers and their possible meaning to you, please turn back to the text and continue reading.

Assuming that you have answered the questions honestly and with objectivity, can you see a pattern of loneliness emerging? If there is a pattern, or profile of your loneliness, examine it carefully to see how it can be combated.

For example, if you are most lonely at night, arrange with a friend or relation with whom you have rapport for a telephone conversation as close as possible to the time of peak loneliness, to which you can look forward each evening. This conversation does not have to be structured or long. Its purpose is only to reaffirm for you that you are not really a solitary soul, functioning in a void of loneliness, but instead are one of billions of human entities, all functioning alone as extensions of one Supreme Being, of whom you are an integral part.

If weekends or holidays are your worst times for loneliness, you are manifesting highly normal symptoms of bereavement. You can use this knowledge to seek reciprocal liaisons with others who live alone: Being together at prearranged times can be as therapeutic for them as it is for you.

You also can try to fill up your most empty days with a schedule of events in which you will participate with others, such as church services, choir practice, amateur theater rehearsals, sports activities, visits to museums, art galleries, or musical events, movies, plays, walks, window-shopping expeditions, or any one or more of dozens of activities that will involve you with others.

If holidays are your darkest times, chances are that Christmas will head the list of days on which you feel most alone—for the earliest and most pleasurable memories for most of us are associated with Christmases we have shared with those we loved, who loved us. Therefore, if a lonely Christmas looms ahead for you, here are a few suggestions that may help: If you have nowhere to go on Christmas, and no one to be with, invite someone to join you in your own celebration. If you are a stranger to your community, or if you do not know anyone you believe might be unattached on Christmas, reveal your need to as many clergymen as it takes to produce a suitable nomination of one to whom your invitation could have meaning. In so doing, the chances also are high that you yourself will receive an invitation to share that holiday's festivities with a family that is reaching out to someone like you.

If all else fails in your efforts to put together or join a joyous Christmas celebration, consider visiting a shut-in or a lonely invalid, whose name you can obtain from your local home health care service.

If your financial resources are not limited, and Christmas and the attendant holidays are a time of trial for you, invite a friend to take a cruise at your expense; or take one alone—for you are bound to meet others on board your ship who have taken the same cruise for the same reasons of loneliness.

If loneliness for you means a special memory, try facing

the memory head-on, giving it as many hours of your time as required for a thorough review. If your first honest effort to let your mind become saturated with this memory is not successful, keep trying—for it is the fragmented, often-avoided recollections that can plague you indefinitely until they are faced for what they are: images from your past, not restrictions on your future.

If you have always been lonely, or if loneliness in your bereavement is pervasive and stays with you all the time, or if your loneliness sometimes leads you to thoughts of self-destruction, you are in need of professional help. To arrange for counseling geared to your ability to pay, contact your local family service agency or mental health clinic.

In sum, to be lonely is to be socially disoriented. Therefore, you may wish to consider the surest cure for loneliness: Become involved in an endeavor designed to help others to ameliorate the trials of living. If you are not sure how and where to make contact with groups devoted to public service on a one-to-one basis, contact your clergyman or the minister of any church, or your United Fund office. Let them know what skills or interests you are willing to share with others, and the first and strongest link in the chain which can bind you to the human race will have been forged. You will be on your way out of the land where each man is an island to a place where everyman's needs are everyman's concern.

If you are the one who brought your marriage to an end, for reasons which, to you, had high validity, your former partner will be feeling *guilt*—but so will you. For no matter what the justification for the severance of your legal ties, you will devote countless hours to second-guessing, to agonizing over the limitless number of *what if*'s that come to your mind. And although this response is to be expected as the result of a broken marriage, there is little psychological profit in it for you.

If you happen to be the partner who was an unwilling party to a divorce action, the guilt you are feeling will deal with the omissions and commissions that caused your mate to wish to end your union—and your *what if*'s can be an endless chain, interwoven with *if only*'s.

In each case (the aggrieved and the aggrievor), the guilt you feel will be a part of the grieving process; until it has been examined and expressed, your healing can not be complete. Therefore, accept your guilt—deserved or undeserved—and know that it should begin to fade away with the memories of the things you did (or did not do), or the things you said (or did not say).

If an honest examination of your guilt feelings leads you to see them as not completely rational or deserved, your time of holding guilt will be lessened. On the contrary, if your assessment of blame justifies an intense feeling of guilt, you can be in for some rough times until you reorder your life in a way that balances out the guilt. To do this, it will be necessary for you to draw from your guilt a pattern or list of personality and character manifestations that caused you to act (or not act) as you did. Possessed of this insight into yourself, you can begin the arduous task of modifying the behavior that led to your divorce.

As your efforts at behavior modification begin to show results, your guilt will give way to growing self-respect. You can begin to look forward with hope to a new life—perhaps with another partner, perhaps alone—in which your efforts to subdue the personal characteristics you find adverse, and emphasize those you perceive as admirable, can lead you to greater happiness in your personal relationships and earlier fulfillment in your chosen work.

If the level of your guilt is extremely high, if your objective assessment of the conduct that caused it leads you to see your guilt as justified, and if your efforts at behavior modification do not bear fruit, you will do well to consider seeking help from your local family service or mental health agency. There you will find professional counselors who are

The Trauma of a Broken Marriage: How to Survive It

able to assist you in understanding the dynamics of your behavior, toward the end of changing it as you desire.

Longing is best defined as a pervasive and free-floating ache that is associated with our deepest emotions. Where reciprocal love has been present in a relationship, longing will exist. It likely will remain, although in muted form and degree, throughout the lifetime of the one who longs—for a heart once freely given remains forever linked with the object which inspired the gift.

If you are feeling the pangs of longing that attend a heartbreaking loss, try to accept your feelings as a tribute to the integrity of your gift of love. Acknowledge them openly to yourself—and to others, if need be.

Recognized as the lasting imprint of another's life upon your own, longing must be accepted as the price one pays for a truly shared life when the sharing ends. If you believe with Elisabeth Kübler-Ross, M.D., and Raymond A. Moody, M.D., that death is but a passage through a dark tunnel to the glorious light at the end, then know that longing is but the force compelling you once more into the presence of those you loved, who await your successful passage to a form of further and expanded sharing.

FEAR QUESTIONNAIRE

1. What things do you fear most? _____
   _____
   _____

2. Is this fear valid? Can it actually happen to you?
   Yes _____ No _____ Maybe _____

3. If your answer is "maybe," what factors can produce your fear? _____
   _____

4. Can you exercise any control over these factors?
   Yes _____ No _____

5. If what you fear does happen, what is the worst thing that can result? _____
   _____
   _____

LONELINESS QUESTIONNAIRE

1. At what time of day and week are you most lonely?
   Morning _____ Evening _____ Night _____
   Weekends _____ .

2. Is this loneliness associated with any particular memory?
   Yes _____ No _____

3. If there is an association, describe it here: _____
   _____

4. If there is no particular association, what triggers your loneliness? _____
   _____

5. Can you think of any way to avoid this trigger? Yes _____
   No _____ . If your answer is "yes," how might you avoid it? _____
   _____

6. Did you feel lonely as a child? Yes _____ No _____

7. If your answer is "yes," when did you stop feeling lonely?
   _____

The Trauma of a Broken Marriage: How to Survive It

8. Were you lonely before your marriage? Yes _____
   No _____

9. Were you ever lonely during your marriage? Yes _____
   No _____

10. If your answer is "yes," in what ways were you lonely, and when were you lonely? _____
    _____
    _____

11. What do you fear most about your loneliness? _____
    _____

12. How valid are these fears? Always very valid _____
    Sometimes valid _____ Seldom valid _____

4
Helping the Bereaved Child

Helping the Bereaved Child

Three out of every five divorces in the USA involve children; more than one-sixth of all children live in single-parent families; and by 1990, it is projected that only 56 percent of all children under the age of eighteen will be living with both natural parents.

Thus, if you are among the nearly eight million women who head families today, you no longer are a member of a minority group once judged by society as disordered, immature, and immoral. Instead, you are beginning to be seen as the fulcrum in a social process of change, based on the fact that whereas a single-parent family can and does exist in many marriages still intact—to the detriment of the children involved—a one-parent household which is well ordered can be a better environment for children who have been vicariously involved in the bickering, anger, and abject hatred that exists in dysfunctional two-parent families.

However, despite the logic of the concept expressed above, the fact remains that children of divorce need special understanding and special help—for a child's heart breaks easily and is especially vulnerable to events over which it has no control. And although it often appears that children recover quickly from emotional shocks, most children simply repress those feelings that they fear and do not understand; they express them later in aberrant behavior.

For this reason, it is important for you as a parent who has experienced divorce, or who may be considering divorce, to learn as much as possible about the cause and pattern of your child's reaction to the trauma of divorce, and to understand what you can do to lessen the depth and duration of your child's emotional response—for next to the loss of a parent by death, the loss of a father or mother by divorce creates a crisis of family transition that produces the most painful distress your child will ever experience.

Although the symptoms of divorce bereavement in children can vary from child to child and family to family, the

Helping the Bereaved Child

principal causes remain constant. They include the following, more or less in this order of importance:

1. Loss of the first and most important sanctuary: the family unit.
2. A move from a familiar home, neighborhood, or city to a new environment.
3. The loss of daily contact with a parent.
4. The disruptions of friendships.
5. Financial fears relating to security.
6. Fear that a parent who left Daddy or Mommy also could abandon him.
7. Feelings of guilt by younger children, whose behavior they perceive as having driven Daddy or Mommy away.
8. Feelings of shame and embarrassment, which are most acute in teenage children.
9. Fear of an unknown future.
10. Fear of coming home to an empty house or apartment (when the parent with custody works away from the home).

If your child's bereavement symptoms include any or all of these causes, they will manifest in various ways, among which the following are most likely to appear according to the age of your child:

Symptoms of Grief in Younger Children

Nervousness
Uncontrollable rages
Frequent sickness
Accident proneness
Antisocial behavior
Rebellious behavior
Hyperactivity
Nightmares
Depression

Symptoms of Grief in Older Children

Difficulty in concentrating
Forgetfulness
Poor schoolwork
Insomnia
Reclusiveness or social withdrawal
Antisocial behavior
Destructive behavior
Resentment of authority
Overdependence
Resistance to discipline
Frequent sickness
Accident proneness
Overeating
Truancy
Experimentation with drugs and/or alcohol
Depression
Secretiveness
Sexual promiscuity
Staying away or running away from home
Talk of or attempted suicide

Of all the behavior changes children can experience, the most predictable response to loss is depression. Normally, the depression of bereavement in children will disappear within a reasonable period of time, and will reflect your own period of grieving. If it continues beyond this time span, depression can be a warning of more serious emotional disturbance, and your child should be evaluated by a mental health practitioner.

As it is with your own bereavement, time usually will greatly modify the manifestation of your child's symptoms. However, if your child is beyond the so-called age of reason (six years), his recollections of the traumas associated with divorce will remain at a subconscious level, available at all times to intrude on his emotional health long beyond the time when he has ceased to express his feelings openly.

Therefore, it is important to your child's emotional stability that you do everything possible to help him overcome his secret fears and anxieties. Among the things you can do to help your child recover from the shock of a changed family unit are the suggestions that follow.

Suggestions for Reducing Your Child's Stress in Bereavement

1. Let your child know that your family relationships have not been terminated, but have simply changed their form.
2. Stress to your child that you and your divorced partner are his or her parents forever—nothing can change that—and that each parent's love will continue.
3. Seek and exploit opportunities for love of your child to be shared by the other parent, and by all of the grandparents.
4. If possible, avoid uprooting your child from familiar surroundings and friends. Try to stay in the same house or apartment, on the same street. Let your child attend the same school for as long as you are able.
5. If you do move, be careful not to discard any of your child's treasures (books, toys, dolls, etc.).
6. Try to stay as close as possible to the familiar routine of living; avoid changes that affect your child.
7. Recognize your child's basic need for security and consistency, and reinforce these feelings at every opportunity.
8. Give your child time to grieve, and accept and share his or her expressions of grief whenever possible.
9. Encourage your child to share feelings of anger, sadness, and fear with you; and respond to them with reassurance and comfort.
10. Let your child know that he or she was not the cause of your divorce.

Helping the Bereaved Child

11. Don't use your child as a go-between or a weapon in dealing with your former mate.
12. Talk positively to your child about the absent parent; help him to love, understand, and respect him or her. Your child needs to feel secure about the worth of both parents.
13. Spend as much time with your child as possible. If you work and your child has an early bedtime, let him or her stay up longer and sleep later, so you both can share that part of the day.
14. Try not to place an inordinate level of responsibility on your child. Assign reasonable chores, but avoid expressing the idea that he or she now is the one who has to take care of Mommy. This can seriously threaten the child's sense of security.
15. Make possible regular visitation with your child's other parent, and help these visitations to be joyful occasions. Children with limited, uncertain, or no contact with a divorced parent suffer the most severe developmental and emotional distress.
16. Listen, *really* listen to your child when he or she talks to you; *look* at him or her during your conversations.
17. Touch and hug your child, hold his or her hand, read to him or her and in every other way possible give your child reassurance of your love and his or her worth.
18. Avoid taking out your anger and frustration on your child.
19. If he or she is young, arrange for your child to have playmates. If he or she is older, encourage friendships with suitable companions.
20. If your child requires day care, be sure it is a good quality of care. Children can survive quite successfully with a surrogate parent who is warm and loving and responsive.
21. Encourage your child to become appropriately independent.
22. Be aware of any sudden or unusual behavior change in

your child which might signify an inordinate level of unresolved stress.
23. On holidays such as Christmas and Thanksgiving, stress that you are a family, and celebrate as a family.
24. Avoid talking about the past with bitterness.
25. Try to look to the future with a positive attitude. Your child will follow your example of coping with courage and confidence.

STEPPARENTING

As four out of every five divorced people remarry, usually within three to five years, and as fifteen million children live at least part-time with stepparents, an important part of dealing with your child's bereavement may involve a new marriage and the expanded stresses it is likely to place on your child. For this reason, it can be of value to you to know in advance some of the emotional hazards of adding a stepparent to your family unit.

Stepparents, like natural parents, bring to marital unions a spectrum of personality configurations, a wide diversity of emotional equipment, and a global difference in environmental backgrounds. Because of these variables in the mental health of stepparents (and their mates), it can be inaccurate to attempt to generalize about stepparents—for some of them bring great happiness to blighted family lives, while others bring emotional chaos.

Nonetheless, there are problems involved with stepparenting that are common to many of the nearly four million revised family structures resulting from second marriages. Those most frequently observed appear below.

Children often resent stepparents, and are jealous of the time and affection they receive from their new mates. Because of this

Helping the Bereaved Child

resentment, children frequently have difficulty relating to stepparents.

Society in general continues to take more of a negative than a positive view toward stepparents. This has an inhibiting effect on their acceptance by children.

A family is the wellspring for emotional support. When the structure of the family changes by the addition of a new adult acting in a parental role, the emotional security of the child can be adversely affected.

Stepfamilies often are beset by jealousies and conflicts of loyalty, which usually are absent in natural families.

Relationships in a natural family evolve and develop slowly, whereas a stepparent becomes a part of the family in one day, by virtue of a marriage service. Thus, the ties of family are impromptu at best; and the relationship between children and stepparent is without the fixed guidelines of habit.

When stepparents join a family unit, conflict with children is always close to the surface. The development of successful family relationships requires a high level of stability, emotional maturity, patience, self-control, and objectivity on the part of the natural parent as well as the stepparent.

When natural parents live in the same community as the stepparent, the role of stepparent is confusing to children, and often in conflict with their feelings.

Where children have regular visitation with a natural parent, conflicts can arise over the difference between the rules and discipline formerly exercised by the biological parent and those established or enforced by the stepparent.

Helping the Bereaved Child

All family structures being unique, it is pretentious and dangerous to offer suggestions for improving family relationships without knowing their nature and the dynamics that may have impaired them. However, having listed problems commonly found in stepfamilies, it may be helpful to propose some ideas for your consideration in dealing with your new role in a family unit that is about to be changed, or has already been changed, by the addition of a stepparent.

Suggestions For Improving Stepparenting Skills

1. If you are now planning to become a stepparent in an existing family, begin to make friends with your future stepchildren as soon as possible. When references to your future role are appropriate, do not say "I'm going to be your new Mommy (or Daddy)." Instead, say "I want to be a part of your family." This will help reduce the inevitable tensions in your relationship with your soon-to-be stepchildren, and will reassure them that their identity as a family unit will be expanded rather than impaired.
2. Partners-to-be in many second marriages encounter financial and psychological stress involving money, which often is related to the payment of child support and alimony. If this condition exists for you, it is important to face and discuss the financial implications of other legal and moral obligations and their potential impact on the proposed union.
3. If your wedding has not taken place, involve the children in its planning; allow them to participate in every way possible.
4. If very young children are involved, postpone your honeymoon until they feel most comfortable with the new family structure. Or if you already have made friends with them and want to be a hero, take them along on your wedding

Helping the Bereaved Child

trip; let them know it is a collective honeymoon, in which a new life will be shared by all.
5. Make friends with your new family by spending time with each child *individually* and with all children as a group several times a week. Use this time to listen and respond to feelings, and to share a game or hobby you can enjoy collectively. This is letting the child enter into your world at his own pace.
6. Move slowly into the role of surrogate parent. Be supportive of existing standards of discipline, and avoid making changes in these rules until you have been accepted as a member of the family unit.
7. Try not to force your relationships. Readjustment takes time. Accept the fact that you can not replace the missing parent, and just be yourself.
8. If a new family unit is being formed, it is advisable to move into another house or apartment in the same neighborhood. This will maintain continuity of environment, but will avoid the feeling and expression by the children that "this is *our* house, not yours!" Also, if possible, allow the children to help choose the new place of residence. This will help them to feel a sense of identity with the new family unit.
9. Avoid changes in routine whenever possible, but be open to requests for changes made by the children.
10. Establish routine family meetings on a periodic basis to discuss and resolve problems and to make or adjust family plans and rules for behavior.
11. Give your partner unquestioned support in the administration of punishment or reprimand; never countermand the request of a natural parent. If you disagree with what is being done, do so after the fact and in private.
12. If both parents bring children to the new union, there is bound to be friction. Expect it, accept it, and work in concert—with the children—to resolve it.

13. In all cases where two families are joined, a certain amount of favoritism is unavoidable. Be on guard against it, and try to avoid it whenever possible.
14. If unresolved and serious conflicts occur in stepfamilies, consider using a local resource for family therapy, in which all members of the family can become involved.
15. As in natural families, most stepfamilies experience personality clashes. For a booklet on how to ease this adjustment, write for "Yours, Mine, Ours" to Consumer Information Center, Dept. 108G, Pueblo, Colorado 81009.

When night falls, the day's work is ended, the children are in bed, and you contemplate with fear and anxiety the long years of potential periodic conflict that lie ahead, be consoled by this thought: The presence of two biological parents in the home is not nearly as important as the presence of two loving adults who present a strong and positive parent image, and who set an example of successful interaction between a man and a woman engaged in life's most challenging role—the raising of a family.

5
Putting Your Life Back Together

Self-Determination After Bereavement

Putting Your Life Back Together

If you are a man who has experienced bereavement, you will share many symptoms with your sisters; but unless you had retired from an active vocational life before your bereavement occurred, you will have the continuity of your work to sustain you and give purpose to your life.

If you are a woman, the chances are less likely that you can focus on a vocation. As of 1979, only 55 percent of all women in the United States over age sixteen were in the work force. Further, if you are a man, it is probable that your earned income is sufficient to release you from the anxieties that attend acute financial pressure. Whereas if you are a woman not employed outside the home, your income may be precarious and inadequate; and if you do have regular outside employment, your earned income will, on the average, be 41 percent lower than the median earnings for men.

Thus, unless you are one of the elite 800,000 women working outside the home who are engaged in a profession, it is likely that your work is not fulfilling or adequately remunerative. Therefore, if you are a bereaved woman, your first goal must be directed toward the attainment of a full life, or a balance between security and excitement.

Unless you happen to be one of the fortunate few—although ever-growing—number of women whose early lives were vocation-directed, you were programmed in childhood to be dependent and nonaggressive, to marry and be taken care of by a man, and to find your fulfillment in serving him in the various roles married women play: wife, mother, mistress, servant, companion. With the ending of these roles through death or divorce, your identity as a wife has come to an abrupt halt. You are faced with the most critical crisis that comes with bereavement: What identity can you now assume?

Many women—especially those who have been widowed in midlife or later—are secure financially; for them, the focus toward fulfillment need not be vocational, unless by choice. A much smaller number of women whose bereavement has followed divorce have adequate financial resources, and can elect to remain apart from the work force. However, even for these two groups of women for whom having enough money is not an issue, the basic question must be answered: "Who am I? To my parents, I was a daughter; to my husband, I was a wife; to my children, I was a mother. But underneath these roles I have played, *what* and *who* am I really?"

In order to find out who you really are, it is necessary to get in touch with your inner self—for there and there only can the answers be found. Today there are a variety of techniques advanced as those that lead to self-knowledge, among them the art of meditation and the discipline of Yoga. And although both these ancient forms of mind and body enrichment have brought many to the end of their search, the Eastern way is not for all. If, in your judgment, they are not for you, you may find the answers you seek in a simpler way, by examining your day-dreams—for it is here, in the inner world of fantasy, that you often can find the key to your ideal vocation. Daydreams are expressions of your inner voice, or intuition, and can provide startlingly clear insight into your secret ambitions for self-fulfillment.

Regardless of your method of focusing on what it is you wish to do to find and express your personal identity, once the early and worst pain of bereavement has subsided, it is important that your first priority become an interest in learning *how* and *where* your energies can be focused to bring you to the attainment of your goal of self-realization.

If you are not possessed of a known learning disability, and if your day-dreams have been of a vocational expression that requires specialized education, go back to school. Each year more and more women whose lives have become displaced by choice or fate have returned to graduate school, to college, or even to high school as a means to the end of finding a self-expression that is interesting and rewarding, as well as financially sustaining.

Putting Your Life Back Together

If one of your inhibitions against returning to school concerns the difference between your age and that of your classmates, be reassured that you will not only not be embarrassed by the experience, but will feel stimulated, renewed, and in every way younger and more vital. Also, today you are sure to find fellow students of all age groups, offering a wide selection of potential friends. It is not unusual for older students who have returned to college to form lasting social relationships with fellow students who are younger, as well as with their peers—for a common educational goal is a strong bond that tends to reduce chronological ages to the median age of the group. This results in a level of social homogeneity which will, in effect, help to restore to you the zest of youth you thought you had lost forever.

If there is any valid reason why a return to school is not possible for you, explore any contacts you may have made as a volunteer, doing work you enjoyed without pay. Very often an avocational expression can be turned into a job that you could enjoy, in an area of service that would add to your self-esteem.

If you happen to be a woman of middle years, whose bereavement is compounded by menopause and the so-called empty nest syndrome, it may be comforting to you to know that thousands of American women each year are successfully changing the focus of their lives from husbands and children to self-expression, or self-actualization. In the process they are finding the antidote to depression and anxiety, and are discovering new levels of happiness and optimism about the future. In short, they are learning that life can be a series of progressions, in which we use change as a catalyst for growth—for although change is often painful, and sometimes involves us in personal crises for which we are totally unprepared, it is only through change that we can find and accept the option to discover our true selves, and be the selves we were meant to be.

On the practical side, if you have never worked outside

Putting Your Life Back Together

your home, and are unable or unwilling to return to school as a bridge to a job that does not involve clerical or service work (which are the occupations of 46 percent of all employed women), you will find that interest, aptitude, and skills testing is available to you at most junior and four-year colleges and universities, as well as at centers for continuing education and private career-counseling firms. If the tests used are comprehensive and properly interpreted, they will be invaluable to you in choosing the vocational field in which you can hope to find your highest level of success and fulfillment.

In addition to these resources, many churches and civic organizations offer career counseling, as does your local CETA office (funded by the federal government, with the full name of Comprehensive Employment and Training Act).

If you are among the majority of bereaved women who are not totally secure financially, you need to be aware of the economic pitfalls that can await you in your new social or legal state. These comprise various forms of financial discrimination, including refusal of credit or delay in receiving it, fictional "requirements" for a second or masculine signature on a lease or loan application, and adverse judgments by credit offices concerning the reliability of alimony and child support payments.

In the past several years many corporations and business firms have begun to issue credit cards in the names of wives as well as husbands. If you possess such cards in your own name, be sure to use them and pay for your charges promptly. However, if no credit was established in your name during your marriage, you will find your husband's charge accounts closed to you; and you are on your own in establishing personal credit.

Unless you are possessed of a fixed income of your own, such as a salary or a trust fund, the best way to establish credit is to open a savings account with a local bank and make regular deposits of sums as large as you can afford. After you have built

Putting Your Life Back Together

up a reasonable balance in your savings account, apply for a short-term loan (for any real or fictitious purpose), and pay off the loan a few days or weeks *before* it comes due.

The next step is to apply to your bank for a credit card (MasterCard or Visa). When issued, it will carry a credit limit based on the amount of money you previously borrowed and repaid and/or the amount in your savings account. As soon as you receive your credit card, begin to use it. And be sure to pay each monthly bill as soon as it arrives. After six months of this sort of credit activity, you will have established a clear credit record. Your subsequent requests to local stores, national oil companies, etc. will favorably reflect your meticulous payment experience, and you will be well on your way to establishing your personal identity as a person of financial responsibility. But a word of warning: A credit card can be a heady thing. When used properly, to charge things for which you have the money to pay, it is a valuable convenience. When used because you can't afford to pay for the article or service you wish to acquire, it can become a potential danger, which can lead to severe financial peril and stress.

If you are divorced (or widowed) and are not living in a home you own, or in which you have an equity, you will be well advised to consider home ownership as your best hedge against inflation. For even with spiraling interest rates, your future economic security may hinge on whether you are at the mercy of endless apartment rent increases, or have made yourself safe against further inflation of housing costs.

Current mortgage rates and housing costs being what they are, the ability of single women to obtain mortgages is not a sure thing, as most banks and savings and loan associations require an annual income of at least $30,000 before approving a mortgage loan for a house in today's lower price range ($65,000). Most single women earn less than this amount.

If the financial logic of owning your own home appeals to you, and you are trapped by the disparity between your current

Putting Your Life Back Together

income and the inflated cost of houses, you may wish to consider teaming up with a friend who is in the same position. If, for example, each of you earns $15,000 a year, you can present a joint mortgage application showing a qualifying income of $30,000. You can become joint owners of a house in which you may wish to live together, or in which your friend has merely made an investment in relation to his or her share of the equity required for the loan approval.

With the advancing liberation of women from various forms of discrimination, you are less likely to be faced today with this sort of business practice. However, if you believe you are being discriminated against because you are the female head of a household, turn for advice and information to your local Department of Citizens' Service and Information (if there is one), the local office of the U.S. Health and Human Services Department, or the Human Rights Advocacy Commission, which is a facility of your state health and rehabilitation service.

Most of us build our lives around a series of milestones that are keyed to timetables such as "after I finish school," "after I'm married," "after the children are grown," "after I achieve some financial independence," or "after I retire." If you are confronted with the unexpected crisis of being without a partner, for you the day has arrived when you must face the need to find the personal meaning of life for you. If you can accept it as an opportunity for self-exploration and self-determination, you will achieve a level of personal freedom beyond your wildest dreams, and you will know the only security worthy of the name: the inner peace and contentment that comes when you learn to know, accept, and express yourself as the unique daughter (or son) of God that you truly are.

In summary, the rebuilding of a life is not an easy task; it is doubly hard when your mind and spirit are filled with grief, remorse, anger, and anxiety. That it can be done is testified to by the legion of valiant women who have accepted and

Putting Your Life Back Together

achieved the opportunity for personal growth that is contained in all adversity. To help yourself attain this growth, try not to look back—for a backward look is an anchor to the past, and it is in the future only that your personal fulfillment can be found.

In your search for this fulfillment in a time of sorrow, recall the words of Kahlil Gibran, who wrote, "Sadness is a wall between two gardens." As you grow in understanding and acceptance of yourself, so grow the chances that for you, a time may come to love again. To bring it closer, close the door to the past (without in any way forgetting what lies there). When you do, a door to the future will open. As it swings wide, you may find it to be a door much like one through which you walked before; or it may be as different a door as can be conceived. But if it opens in response to your knock, there is always the possibility that it will lead to chambers of the heart where you have not dwelled before; and you may find the fruit of your life ripening in the fullness of time.

6
Can Divorce Be Avoided?

Can Divorce Be Avoided?

If you are faced with the possibility of divorce, or have been divorced and are considering another marriage, you may find this chapter of value. For although a cynical lawyer once said that the only way to escape divorce is to abstain from marriage, there are ways in which you can increase your chances of avoiding divorce.

Before considering them, however, it may be useful to examine the anatomy of divorce. Although relatively easy to obtain today, with no-fault and mutual-consent laws available in nearly all states, divorce is seldom sought in haste and without careful thought. Thus, rather than being viewed as an act of severance alone, it can be helpful to see divorce for what it is: a chronological process involving an internal crisis of relationship with one's mate. In this process it is necessary to pass through successive stages, which are five in number.

The first part of the process of divorce is concerned with an intellectual examination of your emotions. In this step you give consideration to the uncertainties involved in change and the anticipation of the loneliness that will follow separation, and you search for less-threatening solutions to your marital dysfunction. At this stage many women choose to avoid the issue by having a child (or another child), by moving to a larger (or different) house or a new neighborhood, by arranging to take a second honeymoon, or by resorting to any one or more of a number of devices designed to reduce the marriage stress, or to postpone acceptance of the disintegrating union.

The second part of the process also is an intellectual one, in which the impact of divorce on your family life, your economic and social life, and your public image is carefully considered. At this stage most women experience strong ambivalence toward their husbands and their marriages.

The third step in the process is a dual one, involving the decision to separate and the act of separation. In marriages where the partner who wants the divorce is possessed of a high level of intellectual honesty, objectivity, and self-control, the

Can Divorce Be Avoided?

third step often is repeated one or more times before the legal system becomes involved.

The fourth part of the process concerns the reorganization of your life, and your struggle to define your separate identity. This stage is made doubly difficult by the lack of clear role models for divorce in our society, with those that do exist being largely negative in nature.

The fifth and last step in the process is devoted to the redefinition of a family unit with a single custodial head, and to consideration of how you can best present your redefined family unit without impairing its acceptance. The fifth step also involves a determination of the relationship of the absent parent with your family, and a structuring of your new family as one with part-time partners involved in decision making concerning children, or one in which the custodial parent receives and accepts full responsibility for the new family unit.

In considering whether or not the dysfunction of your marriage justifies divorce, there are a number of probable results with which you should be familiar. If you have children, these results include the following:

Divorce always creates depression in children, often in those as young as eighteen months. At this age, however, the effect of separation from a parent can be greatly lessened by frequent touching and cuddling your child in love.

If your child is six years old or younger when your family structure is changed, he can experience a loss of trust and confidence which can remain with him throughout life. And if you should be required to leave your home to work, your child will suffer a deeper and more painful loss.

If your child is between the ages of six and twelve at the time of divorce, he will have begun to understand and respond to your

Can Divorce Be Avoided?

reassurance that the new family unit will meet his needs. Nonetheless, he will feel like a helpless bystander observing a wreck.

If your nonadult child is still at home when your marriage is dissolved, the chances are high that he will be conditioned to escape from problems in marriage rather than to seek solutions for them, and his chances for a successful partnership of his own are impaired.

At all ages except infancy, children usually are deeply shocked by the divorce of their parents, and feel that their personal security is threatened. This shock can be greatly lessened by preparing your child for divorce by sharing your decision to end your marriage (after it has been made). However, it is unwise to discuss your reasons for reaching the decision; it can be very harmful if you use this opportunity to impair your child's image or relationship with his father or mother.

If you have not yet reached the first stage in the process of divorce, and have concern about the continuation of your marriage, it may be useful to review some insights concerning the state of matrimony, which may help you to understand the various tensions and stresses that can lead to dissolution. Here are a few of them:

Most divorces occur when the partners are around the age of thirty. The seventh to tenth years of marriage are a time when both partners are most vulnerable to the impulse to escape from the marriage and its bonds.

Most marriages experience midlife crises, usually caused by pressures related to the raising of children, having enough money to meet all family needs and some desires, and/or

Can Divorce Be Avoided?

vocational problems of the wage earner. It is at this time that the second highest number of divorces occur.

Many women of middle age experience severe depression and feelings of inner instability associated with menopause. Today, these psychological and emotional insecurities can be stabilized and controlled chemically; most women can find the relief needed to restore their emotional balance.

Most men, perhaps as high as 75 percent to 80 percent, experience a midlife climacteric, or crisis, of their own. This involves an inner struggle to justify the disparity between their life goals and the attainment of them; to reconcile the work they do with their inner longings or deep-seated desires for self-expression; to accept a diminishing sex drive as a physiological experience rather than a psychological threat to their masculine self-image; to accept the emotional and physical withdrawal of their children at the precise time when interest in them as persons finally has begun to manifest; and to look to the future with optimism and equanimity instead of fear of the uncertainties that the last half of life may hold.

For many men and most women, middle life is a time when the search for personal identity moves from the outside to the inside. Our vision of life takes on new colorations which can affect our emotional responses to our partners. This evolutionary process in a marriage is further complicated by the fact that midlife is a time when many men finally are able to allow their emotions to surface and be expressed in shared communication, while their wives now are less responsive to their husbands' needs, in their own concern with the development at last of a sense of separateness, or selfhood.

Due in great part to the new freedoms of thought and action that the women's liberation movement has produced, many women

Can Divorce Be Avoided?

at midlife are breaking out of long-inhabited domestic cocoons. Coming as they do at the precise time when most men are experiencing strong feelings of futility and unfulfillment, these concurrent evolutionary processes are counterproductive to a halcyon union.

Nearly all woman and most men experience chronological changes in attitudes and feelings as part of the process of living. Unless the changes taking place in each partner are similar, the marriage relationship is subject to stresses that are perceived as threatening, and which can lead to divorce or separation.

All men and women are a combination of masculine and feminine characteristics, with the ideal being a blend of both in each sex. Today, millions of married women are in the process of liberating their aggressive (male) selves, while few men have been willing to explore their female selves. This dichotomy often leads to a level of friction in marriage that can result in divorce.

Knowledge and anticipation of these various threats to the longevity of marriage can be of significant value in overcoming them, as forewarning can help you to accept the changing physical and emotional dynamics of your partner as a part of the process of living a shared life.

In addition, it may be useful to you to realize that all marriages require periodic readjustments; that no marriage contract remains the same, but instead must be renegotiated in midlife; and that happiness in marriage is not found in the absence of problems, but in the commitment to accept and face these problems together and to work in concert to overcome the inevitable crises which are a part of all marriages.

A popular concept about marriage seems to be that sexual problems are a principal cause of most marital stress. And although sex is one cause, it often ranks behind money and communication. However, there are certain aspects of sex in marriage which you should consider in your efforts to avoid divorce; they are set forth below:

For the majority of women, sexual intercourse is an ineffective way to achieve orgasm; there are compelling research studies indicating that perhaps only 30 percent succeed. To find sexual satisfaction, many women resort to masturbation, most of them achieving orgasm. Because of guilt feelings stemming from our collective puritanical heritage, many women are ashamed of this natural act. It may help you to know that one national study shows that 82 percent of all women find periodic release through masturbation.

Despite the great stress put on orgasm today, it is not always the most important part of sex for many women, for whom the deepest fulfillment comes only from mutual relating, sharing, and caring.

Sexual problems in marriage often stem from a lack of communication between partners, due to inhibition against being explicit about sex needs, desires, and fantasies. Only by telling your mate what pleases you can you attain the level of true intimacy on which most successful marriages are based.

Men in their twenties have higher sex drives than their marriage partners in the same age group. However, as they reach middle years, most men experience a drop in libido, while the sex desire of their mates generally becomes more active. As libido in men is closely related to their masculine self-image, the most successful middle-age unions are those in which the female partner handles the problem of a reverse differential in the need for sex with insight, delicacy, and tact, being careful not to make demands that can not be met.

Can Divorce Be Avoided?

The personal psychological problems of either partner can be responsible for the diminishment of sex drive and other sex difficulties in marriage. If you believe such problems exist, it is wise to consider counseling by a qualified practitioner.

A significant weight gain by either partner can result in a marked change in sexual attractiveness. To maintain a satisfactory level of attraction, many women and men whose marriages remain successful take care of their bodies through appropriate diet and regular exercise.

Couples with a deep and stable emotional relationship usually maintain a consistent level of mutual sex interest and response throughout their marriage. However, it should be kept in mind that interest can be responsive to the feeling of emotional distance that either partner can experience from time to time.

Problems in marriage concerning money can be frequent. And although the stresses of inflation are causing more couples to be concerned today about their level of income, the amount of money available to a husband and wife is not as important as whether all income is disposed of for living and recreation. Because of this, couples with moderate incomes who have a fixed savings or investment plan, and who live well within their incomes, have a much greater chance for long and happy unions than couples with large incomes that are overcommitted.

The second most frequently encountered problem about money in marriage is deciding how it will be spent. Where such decisions are made principally by the husband, trouble is bound to result; many middle-years marriage breakups can be traced to the slowly building and eventual exploding of a wife's resentment at her lack of control over how the family income is disposed of. If your marriage is one in which money cannot be

Can Divorce Be Avoided?

budgeted adequately, or is controlled entirely by the husband, counseling about the handling of money can go a long way to save it from faltering and ending in divorce.

Even with a satisfactory level of mutual sexual satisfaction and shared agreement on the prudent use of family income, all marriages can be enriched by increased knowledge and use of communications skills between partners. Among those techniques that can be helpful in building a better relationship with your partner, the following ideas may be of the most value to you:

Happy and successful marriages do not just happen. They result from a mutual willingness by both partners to work together toward a life that is truly satisfying for *each* partner.

An important factor in the attainment of a successful marriage is a willingness on the part of both partners to discuss and agree on the roles each partner will play in the marriage. This often is easier for younger people than for those who have long been exposed to stereotypical masculine and feminine roles as a part of their social environment.

In order to produce a mutually satisfying life, it is necessary to learn to share yourself with your partner. Successful sharing requires the mutual revealing of your hopes and dreams, your fears and concerns, your joys and sorrows; above all, it requires that you *listen* to your partner with empathy, respond with an open and caring heart, and attempt to understand and meet his or her needs.

In your communication with your partner, try to distinguish between issues and problems. Issues can be anything that relates to a marriage, such as changes of any kind—a new job, a new child, a new home. Issues also can involve feelings of

Can Divorce Be Avoided?

dissatisfaction with your partner, or unexpected life events. Issues only become problems when they are not identified as issues, are not faced, or are unresolved.

In dealing with issues in a marriage, *what* you say to your partner is less important than *how, when,* and even *where* you say it.

In communicating with your partner, it is important to understand the differences between statements that express your thoughts and those which express your feelings. For example, if you say "I think you are upset," this reflects only your judgment or understanding of your partner's actions. However, if you say "I feel threatened when I think you are upset," this reveals to your partner how your interpretation of his or her actions makes you feel.

Successful communication between partners is based on mutual awareness, which can only come about by attentive listening and observing. To accomplish this, it is helpful to give your full attention to your partner when he or she is speaking to you, to maintain eye contact whenever possible, and to be responsive to his revelations of feelings by sharing your own.

In dealing with your partner, try to avoid confrontation. For example, if your husband is two hours late getting home, instead of saying "Why didn't you let me know you'd be late?" try "You must have run into an unexpected situation to be so late. Is everything OK?"

In communicating with your partner, be sure that he or she not only understands what you have said, but also comprehends the meaning behind it. Often this can best be accomplished by repeating your statement and adding a simple definition of your meaning. For example, if your first statement is "I'm ready for bed," your follow-up statement might be "I'm not really that sleepy, but I feel like being loving with you."

Successful communication with your partner not only involves voice and eye contact, but also includes physical contact. Touching can modify a statement which, without tender physical contact, could be misinterpreted. For example, if a woman is disturbed about something her partner has done (or said), she might say from across the room, "How many times have I asked you not to do (or say) that!" But if she walked over to her partner, put her arms around him, and said "I love you, you big ox! But how many times do I have to ask you not to say (or do) that," the effect of her words has been modified and reinforced at the same time, and she probably has avoided the conflict that would have resulted from her first approach.

Achieving and maintaining a successful marriage is never easy, and sometimes requires help from others. The French writer Alexander Dumas once offered the opinion that "The bonds of matrimony are so heavy it sometimes takes three to carry them." He was referring, of course, to the time-honored French custom of an illicit sex liaison by one (or both) partners. And although there are those practitioners of sexual promiscuity who claim that variety in sexual partners has strengthened their marriage, and there also are psychologists who would agree with Dumas, that is not the opinion of this writer.

However, taking Dumas's clever statement out of context, there *are* times when it does take three to carry the heavy chains of matrimony. The third party would be a trained counselor, who can serve as a catalyst in helping distressed and dysfunctional marriage partners to understand the causes of their stress and to modify the attitudes or behavior helping to produce it.

Can Divorce Be Avoided?

If you believe that your marriage can be helped by counseling, contact your local family service agency, where you will find well-trained and knowledgeable marriage and family counselors who can guide you in understanding your own feelings and responses, and can help you to bring about favorable changes in your relationship with your mate. However, to be successful, marriage counseling should involve both partners; the unwillingness of your mate to participate could signify a deeper level of psychological stress, which could point to the ultimate need for more skilled and prolonged personal counseling.

In summary, not all marriages can be saved; some marriage partners and their children would be better off if divorce ensued. Nonetheless, it is safe to say that most marriages can be helped and prolonged by the willingness of partners to work in concert to accomplish mutually acceptable goals for their relationship and their lives together.

As Philip Goldberg has written, the Chinese character for crisis is a combination of the words *danger* and *opportunity*. No better thought could be found to express the elements inherent in the crisis of an unstable marriage—for at worst, it is fraught with unnumbered perils; at best, it presents an opportunity to use the fabric of two lives to weave a tapestry of unparalleled beauty. Although a partnership between a man and a woman is not for all, for most of us life is not worth the candle unless its light can be shared.

7
The Single Life

Its Joys and Sorrows

The Single Life: Its Joys and Sorrows

The word *single* in the context of people has different connotations. To the unhappily married person, *single* can stand for blessed release from the chains of matrimony. To the well-adjusted, successful, career-oriented woman, *single* can mean freedom to live her own life without interference. However, for all who are single, a life lived alone can have advantages as well as disadvantages. Which outweighs the other will depend in great part on the personality and mental and physical health of the person living alone, as well as on whether the decision to live alone is voluntary or involuntary.

For those who are not living alone by choice, a single state can lead to problems and perils, as well as terrors, which include the following:

A feeling of being stunned, or paralyzed, if suddenly forced by circumstances to change from a life of companionship to one in which there is no one to share your problems, help you make decisions, or to care whether you live or die.

Being sick when you are alone and have no one to care for you or give you sympathy.

Especially if you are a woman, the social pressure to marry, and the emotional pressure to couple.

The thought of growing old alone, with no one to care for you in infirmity.

If you are a woman who works in a relatively low-level job, the responsibility of meeting your own living expenses and financial obligations.

For single women, the potential trap of multiple sex partners, which can lead to unwanted pregnancy, venereal disease, social disapproval, and lowered self-esteem.

The Single Life: Its Joys and Sorrows

For all people living alone, an increased incidence of heart attacks, lung cancer, strokes, influenza, and pneumonia. For men living alone, cirrhosis of the liver and tuberculosis are likely threats.

For most single people, the risk of a level of social isolation, which can lead to severe emotional stresses. There is a biological basis for the need to form human relationships. When this need is not met, physical deterioration can follow, resulting in generally impaired health.

Of all the trials of a single life, the most universal is loneliness. And although loneliness often is present in marriage, when it results from an unwilling single state, it is pervasive and intense; according to the weight of psychiatric authority, loneliness also can result in death. Seen in this light by lay persons as well as professionals in the field of mental health, loneliness is decried by W. H. Auden, the English poet, when he writes "We must love one another or die." Extensive research concerning loneliness has led James J. Lynch, M.D., of the University of Maryland School of Medicine, to report dialogue with another person as the most essential element in overcoming loneliness. He sees verbal interaction between two people as "the elixir of life itself."

If loneliness is prolonged, depression results, and the process of human deterioration is accelerated. Most severe depressions are related to an extreme lack of human contact, and although ours is a country known the world over for its open, gregarious, and friendly nature, a Gallup Poll of 1980 revealed that 10 percent of our citizens have only one or two friends, and 3 percent have no friends at all.

Removing loneliness and depression from the life of a single person is not always easy, and sometimes is impossible. Nonetheless, these two scourges of mental and physical well-being can be combated with some success by following the suggestions below.

Ideas For Overcoming Loneliness And Depression

For obvious reasons, friendships must be formed; the suggestions advanced in Chapters 2 and 3 of this book can be useful to you in developing social situations from which friendships can flow.

Try to maintain at least one solid, dependable social base in your life. If you have relatives with whom you are compatible, their home can serve this purpose well; annual or other periodic visits should be made for the purpose of reaffirming your social roots and restoring your sense of identity. If you have no relatives who can meet this need, the home of an old and close friend can serve the same purpose. No matter how far the distance from your friend, it is important that your visits be regular and no less frequent than once a year. The very process of planning and being able to look forward to such visits will go far toward relieving your loneliness and depression.

As loneliness and depression bring responsive physical stress, you can combat them more successfully if you take care to build and maintain a high level of physical energy. This can be done by following a planned exercise program—indoors or out—and steadily increasing the amount of exercise until your body has responded with a new vitality. You also can improve your physical condition by eating three times a day (only), and by avoiding or cutting down on your use of coffee, cigarettes, stimulants, tranquilizers, and alcohol (which will bring you early relaxation, but later depression; when used to excess at night, nearly always results in early-morning wakefulness).

The Single Life: Its Joys and Sorrows

If you happen to be plagued by insomnia (as most lonely and depressed people are), this program of exercise and controlled diet is sure to help you to experience longer and deeper sleep.

Nighttime is known to be the most successful enemy of a tranquil spirit in those who live alone; and it deserves special consideration. To overcome the loneliness which comes in the dark and quiet of the night, make your bedroom (or your bed) a pleasant place to use as your retreat, being sure that your sleeping needs are as well met as possible, and that you have a good reading light, an interesting book, a radio, a clock and a flashlight by your bed. When sleep won't come—for whatever reason—and you are bored with reading, get up and accomplish some special task you have been putting off. Not only will this effort expend physical and emotional energy, but the virtuous feeling that comes from completing a task you have been avoiding will give you a feeling of euphoria, which is easily transferred into restful slumber.

If your efforts to combat loneliness and depression are unsuccessful at any point, and if you feel like you will explode from anxiety, call your local hot line, or crisis center for instant telephone contact with another person who has volunteered to receive, listen, and respond to the calls of lonely people in distress.

According to a 1980 Gallup survey, 74 percent of America women will choose marriage and children over a single life. However, for those who prefer to be single, or who find an unexpected solo act to be to their liking, the advantages most often mentioned by women living alone are these:

Pride in directing your own life, in being in control of yourself and your destiny, in making your own decisions without a hassle, and in coping with life successfully.

The Single Life: Its Joys and Sorrows

Although loneliness can impair happiness as a single person, living alone is infinitely preferable to being caught in an unhappy marital relationship.

The freedom of responsibility for the contentment of another person; the lack of pressure to please someone else, or pay a penalty for not doing so.

The excitement of being free to move in any social direction you choose, without criticism or obstruction.

The opportunity to form an infinite number of social relationships without impairing any one of them; the freedom from possessive jealousy.

The freedom to live at your own pace, in a place of your own choosing; sleeping and eating when you please and with whom you please.

Freedom to focus your energies on a fulfilling and rewarding career, without restrictive obligations to another person.

Freedom to visit friends of your choice, when you wish, without regard to the prejudices, likes, and dislikes of another.

Freedom to accept travel invitations; the excitement of making your own travel decisions and experiencing travel uninhibited by the needs, desires, and prejudices of another.

Freedom to live as you please; be dressed or undressed as you wish; be neat or slovenly, as the spirit moves; be hot or cold, without regard for the comfort of anyone else.

Freedom to listen to music of your choice, when and for as long as you wish to hear it.

The Single Life: Its Joys and Sorrows

Freedom to furnish and decorate your home to your own taste, without compromise with another.

There was a time, not too long ago, when a man and woman sharing the same living space were considered to be living in sin. No more. Today, more than two million couples are known to be living together without benefit of clergy, an increase of over 100 percent since 1970; and the trend toward a shared life without marriage shows no signs of decreasing its rate of acceleration. The advantages of such an arrangement are numerous, with the principal ones appearing below.

Companionship without commitment.

The support of sharing problems and decisions without being faced with long-term obligations.

Freedom to develop a life-style and a relationship which (usually) is not threatened by the presence of children.

Avoidance of the consideration to raise a family and incur the ever-increasing expense of child rearing, placed by the Urban Institute at $85,000 in 1980 for out-of-pocket expenses to see a middle-class child from birth (which now costs $3,000 alone) through a public university.

Freedom from the emotional obligations and behavior problems attendant on dealing with offspring, who are essentially self-centered, and from whom little comfort can be expected.

Freedom to achieve autonomy in intimacy, without giving up yourself.

As marriage is less about love than possession, the freedom to develop a loving relationship without the restriction of possessiveness.

The Single Life: Its Joys and Sorrows

Despite the above advantages of sharing a life without taking marriage vows, for most who choose it, such a relationship is an open-ended way station on the road to matrimony, as 95 percent of all Americans have been married or will marry at some point in their lives. Therefore, for those who see an unwedded state as a threat to the social security of our nation, it may be comforting to know that the financial obligations of an unwedded companionship, which the celebrated Lee Marvin case has firmly fixed as a point of law, will no doubt serve as an inhibiting factor to the formation of long-term liaisons. This fact, coupled with the nature of man to find permanence in sharing, will assure well the continuation of the race without impairment. And it will, in time, be understood that all societies must move through all levels of freedom of choice en route to the ultimate surrender of self to the advance of mankind through the exaltation of the spirit.

Bibliography

Grief and Bereavement Resulting from Death

Agee, James. *A Death in the Family.* New York: Avon, 1963.

Arthur, Bettie, and Mary Kemme. "Bereavement in Childhood." *Journal of Child Psychology and Psychiatry* 5 (June 1964), 37–49.

Barry, Herbert, Jr., Herbert Barry, and Erich Lindemann. "Dependency in Adult Patients Following Early Maternal Bereavement." *Journal of Nervous and Mental Diseases* 140 (March 1965), pp. 196–206.

Becker, Howard. "The Sorrow of Bereavement." *Journal of Abnormal and Social Psychology* 27 (March 1933), pp. 391–410.

Benda, Clemens. "Bereavement and Grief Work." *Journal of Pastoral Care* 16 (Spring 1962), pp. 1–13.

Bowlby, John. "Processes of Mourning." *International Journal of Psychoanalysis* 42, 4–5 (1961), pp. 317–40.

———. *Attachment and Loss.* Vol. 1, *Attachment* (1969); Vol. 2, *Separation, Anxiety and Anger* (1973). London: Hogarth.

——— "Disruption of Affectional Bonds and Its Effects on Behavior." *Journal of Contemporary Psychotherapy* 2 (Winter 1970), pp. 75–86.

Clayton, Paula J. "Mortality and Morbidity in the First Year of Widowhood." *Archives of General Psychiatry* 30 (June 1974), pp. 747–50.

Clayton, Paula J., James A. Halikas, William L. Maurice, and Eli Robbins. "Anticipatory Grief and Widowhood." *British Journal of Psychiatry* 122 (January 1973), pp. 47–51.

Clayton, Paula J., James A. Halikas, and William L. Maurice. "The Depression of Widowhood." *British Journal of Psychiatry* 120 (January 1972), pp. 71–77.

Cryer, Newman S. and John M. Vayhinger. *Caseload in Pastoral Counseling.* New York: Abington Press, 1962.

Das, S. Sunder. "Grief and Imminent Threat of Non-Being." *British Journal of Psychiatry* 118 (April 1971), pp. 467–68.

———. "Grief and Suffering." *Psychotherapy: Theory, Research, and Practice* 8 (Spring 1971): pp. 8–9.

Bibliography

Deutsch, Helene. "Absence of Grief." *Psychoanalytic Quarterly* 6 (January 1937), pp. 12–22.

Eliot, Thomas D. "The Bereaved Family." *Annals of American Academy of Political and Social Science* 160 (March 1932), pp. 184–90.

———. "The Adjusted Behavior of Bereaved Families: A New Field of Research." *Social Forces* 8 (June 1932), pp. 543–45.

Freud, Sigmund. *Mourning and Melancholia: Collected Papers.* New York: Basic Books, 1959.

Fulconer, David M. "The Adjustive Behavior of Some Recently Bereaved Spouses: A Psycho-Sociological Study." Ph.D. dissertation, Northwestern University, 1942.

Glaser, Barney, *Awareness of Dying.* Chicago: Aldine Publishing Co., 1965.

Glick, Ira O., Robert S. Weiss, and C. Murray Parkes. *The First Year of Bereavement.* New York: John Wiley and Sons, 1974.

Gorer, G. *Death, Grief and Mourning.* London: Cresset Press, 1965.

Harrison, S. I. "In Children's Reactions to Bereavement: Adult Confusion and Misperceptions." *Archives of General Psychiatry* 17 (March 1967), pp. 593–97.

Headlee, Judith Anne. "Let Grieving Go." *The Single Parent* (October 1975), pp. 12–13.

Hodge, John. "Social Work and the Mourning Parent." *Social World* 7 (January 1972), pp. 25–36.

Howard, Jane. *A Different Woman.* New York: E. P. Dutton and Co., 1973.

Kastenbaum, Robert J. and R. B. Aisenberger. *The Psychology of Death.* New York: Springer, 1972.

Klein, Melanie. "Mourning and Its Relationship to Manic Depressive States." *International Journal of Psycho-Analysis* 21 (April 1940), pp. 121–153.

Kobler, Arthur L. and Ezra Stotland. *The End of Hope.* New York: Free Press, 1964.

Lewis, C. S. *Grief Observed.* New York: Seabury Press, 1963.

Lindemann, Eric. "The Symptomology and Management of Acute Grief." *American Journal of Psychiatry* 100 (May 1944), pp. 101–41.

Lopata, Helen Z. *Widowhood in an American City.* Cambridge, Mass.: Schenkman Publishing, 1973.

Love, Ann. "The Widow's Study." *The Single Parent* (October 1974), pp. 28–37.

Maddison, D. "The Consequences of Conjugal Bereavement." *Nursing Times* 65 (January 9, 1969), pp. 50–52.

Bibliography

Marris, Paul. *Widows and Their Families.* London: Routledge and Kogan Paul, 1958.

———. *Loss and Change.* London: Routledge and Kogan Paul, 1974.

Moss, S., and M. Moss. "Long-Term Adaption of the Elderly to Bereavement." *Journal of Gerontology* 28 (July 1973), pp. 359–62.

Parkes, Collin Murray. *Bereavement: Studies of Grief in Adult Life.* New York: International Universities Press, 1972.

Parkes, Collin Murray, and R. J. Brown. "Health After Bereavement: A Controlled Study of Young Boston Widows and Widowers," *Psychosomatic Medicine* 34 (September–October 1972), pp. 449–61.

Parkes, Collin Murray, Ira O. Glick, and Robert S. Weiss. *The First Year of Bereavement.* New York: John Wiley and Sons, 1974.

Perske, Robert. "Death and Ministry: Episode and Response." *Pastoral Psychology,* No. 15 (1964), pp. 25–35.

"Plight of America's Two Million Widowers." *U.S. News and World Report,* (April 15, 1974), pp. 49–52.

Pollock, George H. "Anniversary Reactions, Trauma and Mourning." *Psychoanalytic Quarterly* 39 (July 1970), pp. 347–51.

———. "Bertha Pappenheim's Pathological Mourning: Possible Effects of Childhood Sibling Loss." *Journal of the American Psychoanalytic Association* 20 (July 1972), pp. 476–93.

———. "On Time, Death, and Immortality." *Psychoanalytic Quarterly* 40 (July 1971), pp. 435–46.

Priest, R. G. and A. H. Crisp, "Bereavement and Psychiatric Symptoms: An Item Analysis." *Psychotherapy and Psychosomatics* 22 (1973), pp. 166–71.

Rush, Benjamin. *Medical Inquiries and Observations Upon the Diseases of the Mind.* Philadelphia: Kimber and Richardson, 1812.

Salom, Francisco. "Surviving Widowhood." *The Single Parent* (May 1974), pp. 29–33.

Schoenberg, B., ed. *Anticipatory Grief.* New York: Columbia University Press, 1974.

Silverman, Phyllis R. "The Widow to Widow Program." *Mental Hygiene* 53 (July 1969), pp. 333–37.

Stinette, Charles R. *Anxiety and Faith.* New York: Seabury Press, 1955.

Vernick, Joel. *A Bibliography of Death.* Washington: National Institute of Mental Health, 1968.

Webster's Seventh New Collegiate Dictionary. Springfield, Mass.: G. & C. Merriam Co., 1970.

Bibliography

Weiss, Robert S. *Loneliness: The Experience of Emotional and Social Isolation.* Cambridge, Mass.: Massachusetts Institute of Technology Press, 1973.

Weissman, Avery D. *On Death and Dying.* New York: Behavioral Publications, 1972.

Divorce

Allen, Nathan. "Divorce in New England." *North American Review* 130 (June 1880), p. 560.

Arieti, Silvano, ed. "Reactions to Divorce." *Psychological Aspects of Divorce.* New York: Basic Books, 1974.

Bartlett, George A. *Men, Women and Conflict.* New York: G. P. Putnam's Sons, 1931.

Bel Geddes, Joan. "Adjusting Yourself: The Transition from Grief to Peace." *The Single Parent* (January/February 1975), pp. 39–41.

Blake, Nelson M. *The Road to Love: A History of Divorce.* New York: Macmillan Co., 1962.

Bohannon, Paul. *Divorce and After.* Garden City: Doubleday, 1970.

———. "The Six Stations of Divorce." *The Single Parent* (January/February 1971), pp. 28–31.

Bova, Ben and Barbara Berson. *Survival Guide for the Suddenly Single.* New York: St. Martin's Press, 1974.

Brandewein, R. A., C. A. Brown, and E. M. Fox. "Women and Children Lost: The Social Liberation of Divorced Mothers and Their Families." *Journal of Marriage and the Family* 35 (April 1974), pp. 498–514.

Briscoe, C. "Depression and Marital Turmoil." *Archives of General Psychiatry* 29 (December 1973), pp. 811–17.

Briscoe, C. and J. Smith. "Psychiatric Illness: Marital Upsets and Divorce." *Journal of Nervous and Mental Diseases* 158 (June 1974), pp. 440–44.

Brown, Emily M., ed. *Report of the Task Force on Divorce and Divorce Reform.* Minneapolis: National Council on Family Relations, 1974.

Burr, W. R. *Theory Construction and the Sociology of the Family.* New York: Wiley, 1973.

Cantor, Donald J. *Escape From Marriage.* New York: William Morrow, 1971.

Carter, H. and P. C. Glick. *Marriage and Divorce: A Social and Economic Study.* Cambridge, Mass.: Harvard University Press, 1970.

Champagne, Marian. *Facing Life Alone: What Widows and Divorcees Should Know.* New York: Bobbs-Merrill Co., 1964.

Cowan, Connel O. "Twisted Reflections, Healthy Perceptions." *Marriage and Divorce* (August 1974), pp. 19–23.

Bibliography

Cowley, Charles. *Divorce Courts: Their Origin and History.* Lowell, Mass.: Penhallow Printing Co., 1879.

Cuse, Arthur, *Financial Guidelines: Divorce.* Los Angeles: Guideline Publishing Co., 1975.

Desmond, Charles S. "The Annulment Problem," *New York State Bar Association Bulletin* 20 (April 1948), pp. 59–65.

Edwards, Marie and Eleanor Hoover. *The Challenge of Being Single.* New York: Hawthorne, 1974.

Epstein, Joseph. *Divorced in America.* New York: E. P. Dutton, 1974.

Ernst, Morris L., and David Loth. *For Better or Worse: A New Approach to Marriage and Divorce.* New York: Harper & Bros., 1952.

Ewing, Stephen. "The Mockery of American Divorce." *Harpers* (July 1928), pp. 49–54.

Fisher, Esther Oshiver. *Divorce: The New Freedom.* New York: Harper & Row, 1974.

Fuller, Jan. *Space: The Scrapbook of My Divorce.* New York: Arthur Fields Books, 1973.

Gardner, Richard A. *The Boys and Girls Book About Divorce.* New York: Science House, 1970.

Gettleman, Susan and Janet Markowitz. *The Courage to Divorce.* New York: Simon & Schuster, 1974.

Glick, Paul C. "Marital Stability as a Social Indicator." *Social Biology* 16 (March 1969), pp. 158–66.

Goode, William J. *Women in Divorce.* New York: Free Press, 1956.

Green, Leslie. "Why I Miss Being Married." *Woman's Day* (November 1975), p. 51.

Grollman, E. A., ed. *Explaining Divorce to Children.* Boston: Beacon Press, 1969.

Hallett, Kathryn. *A Guide for Single Parents.* Millbrae, Calif.: Celestial Arts, 1973.

Harrell, Pat. *Divorce and Remarriage in the Early Church.* R. B. Sweet Co., 1967.

Hicks, Mary W. and Marilyn Platt. "Marital Happiness and Stability: A Review of the Research in the Sixties." *Journal of Marriage and the Family* 32 (November 1970), pp. 553–74.

Hirsch, Barbara B. *Divorce: What a Woman Needs to Know.* Chicago: Henry Regnery Co., 1975.

Hunt, Morton. *The World of the Formerly Married.* New York: McGraw-Hill, 1966.

Bibliography

Jacobson, Paul H. *American Marriage and Divorce*. New York: Rinehart & Co., 1959.

Johnson, Janet. "Journey of a Divorcee." Cosmopolitan (April 1975), pp. 68–84.

Johnson, Walter D. "An Experiment in Education." *The Single Parent* (October 1975), pp. 32–36.

Kapit, Hannah. "The Widowed and the Divorced." *The Single Parent* (September 1969), pp. 21–27.

Kelleher, Stephen J. *Divorce and Remarriage for Catholics*. Garden City, N.Y.: Doubleday and Co., 1973.

Kessler, Sheila. *The American Way of Divorce: Prescription for Change*. Chicago: Nelson-Hall, 1975.

Klein, Carole. *The Single Parent Experience*. New York: Walker and Co., 1973.

Koster, Donald W. *The Theme of Divorce in American Drama*. Philadelphia: University of Pennsylvania, 1949.

Kraft, Thomas. "Solitude or Loneliness." *The Single Parent* (January/February 1974), pp. 25–30.

Krantzler, Mel. *Creative Divorce*. New York: M. Evans & Co., 1973.

Landgraf, J. "Reasons for Marriage Breakdown: A Case Study in Southwestern Ontario (Canada)." *Journal of Comparative Family Studies* 2 (Fall 1971), pp. 226–51.

Leader, Arthur L. "Family Therapy for Divorced Fathers and Others Out of Home." *Social Casework* 54 (January 1973), pp. 13–19.

_____. "Divorce and Psychiatric Diseases." *Archives of General Psychiatry* 29 (July 1973), pp. 119–25.

Levinger, George. "Sources of Marital Dissatisfaction Among Applicants for Divorce." *American Journal of Orthopsychiatry* 36 (1966), pp.347–80.

Lobos, R. "A Guide to Divorce Counseling." *Family Coordinator* 22 (January 1973), pp. 55–61.

Lyman, Howard B. *Single Again*. New York: David McKay, 1971.

Markowitz, Janet and Susan Gettleman. *The Courage to Divorce*. New York: Simon & Schuster, 1974.

McKenney, Mary. *Divorce: A Selected Annotated Bibliography*. Metuchen, N.J.: Scarecrow Press, 1975.

Martin, John R. *Divorce and Remarriage: A Perspective for Counseling*. Scottsdale, Pa.: Herald Press, 1974.

Melman, Carla. "Divorce: A Community Affair." *The Single Parent* (April 1974), pp. 49–51.

Bibliography

Metz, Charles V. *Divorce and Custody for Men.* Garden City, N.Y.: Doubleday, 1968.

Mindey, Carol. *The Divorced Mother.* New York: McGraw-Hill, 1969.

O'Brien, Patricia. *The Woman Alone.* New York: Quadrangle New York Times Book Co., 1974.

O'Donovan, Barbara. "The Stages of Divorce." *The Single Parent* (May 1969), pp. 72–75.

O'Neill, D. "Open Marriage: Implications for Human Service Systems." *Family Coordinator* 22 (April 1973), pp. 449–56.

O'Sullivan, Sonya. "Single Life in a Double Bed." *Harpers* (November 1975), p. 45.

Ploscowe, Morris. *The Truth About Divorce.* New York: Hawthorne Books, 1955.

Polatin, Phillip and Ellen C. Philtine. "Divorce: From the Man's View." *The Single Parent*, November 1974, pp. 21–26.

———. "After Divorce: Another Marriage?" *The Single Parent* (July/August 1975), pp. 63–67.

Reed, Angela. *The Woman on the Verge of Divorce.* England: Plume Press Ltd., and Ward Lock Ltd., 1960.

Rheinstein, Max. *Marriage Stability, Divorce and the Law.* Chicago: University of Chicago Press, 1972.

Schlesinger, Benjamin. *The One-Parent Family: Perspectives and Annotated Bibliography.* Toronto: University of Toronto Press, 1970.

———. "The Death of a Marriage." *The Single Parent* (May 1974), pp. 19–22.

Scott, Helen, "From Trauma to Triumph." *The Single Parent* (October 1974), pp. 58–60.

Sheresky, Norman and Marya Mannes. *Uncoupling. The Art of Coming Apart.* New York: Viking Press, 1972.

Singleton, Mary Ann. *Life After Marriage.* New York: Stein & Day, 1974.

Steinzor, Bernard. *When Parents Divorce.* New York: Pantheon, 1969.

Stewart, Suzanne. *I Wouldn't Have Given a Nickel for Your Chances.* Grand Rapids, Mich.: Zondervan Publishing, 1974.

Symonds, M. "Marital Disharmony and Character Structure." *American Journal of Psychoanalysis* 30 (January 1970), pp. 73–86.

Taves, Isabelle. *Woman Alone.* New York: Funk and Wagnalls, 1968.

United Nations Department of Economic and Social Affairs. Statistical Office. United Nations: New York, 1975.

Bibliography

Waller, Willard. *The Old Love and the New: Divorce and Readjustment.* Carbondale, Ill.: Southern Illinois University Press, 1967 (initially published in 1930).

Westermarck, Edward. *The History of Human Marriage,* 5th ed. New York: Allerton Book Co., 1922.

Wheeler, Michael. *No-Fault Divorce.* Boston: Beacon Press, 1974.

Whitaker, C. A. and Milton H. Miller. "A Reevaluation of 'Psychiatric Help' When Divorce Impends." *American Journal of Psychiatry* 126 (May 1969), pp. 611–18.

Index

Abandonment, feeling of, 3
Anger, 3
   in depression, 20
   as symptom of divorce, 30, 33–34
Anxiety, 3
   as symptom of divorce, 30–32
Appetite, loss of, 3
Auden, W. H., 79

Career counseling, 61
Census Bureau, U.S., 22
CETA (Comprehensive Employment and Training Act), 61
Children, 46–55
   cost of raising, 83
   custody of, male vs. female attitudes to loss of, 6
   lonely divorced people with, 36–37
   offsetting stress of divorce bereavement in, 49–51
   reactions to divorce of, 67–68
   stepparenting, 51–55
   symptoms of divorce bereavement in, 46–49
Christmas, 38
Church, 12
   loneliness and, 36
   widow's support from, 10–11
   See also Religion
Citizens' Service and Information Department, 63
Communication problems in marriage, 73–75
Condominiums, 15–17
Consumer Information Center, 55
Counseling
   career, 61
   marriage, 75–76

Couples living together, 22, 83
Credit, establishing, 61–62
Crying, 20

Death
   psychological preparation for, 6–7
   of spouse, stress rating of, 29
Denial of loss, 3
Dependency in depression, 20
Depression, 3
   coping with, 20–23
   as effect of divorce on children, 67
   loneliness and, 19, 23, 79
   menopausal, and marital stress, 69
   professional help for, 22
   single life and, 79–81
   symptoms of, 19–20
   in widows, 19–20, 23
   See also Grief
Desertion, incidence of, 28
Despair, 3
   in depression, 20
Discrimination against women, financial, 63
Divorce
   age of occurrence of, 68–69
   children and statistics on, 46
   chronological stages of, 66–67
   male vs. female attitudes toward, 6
   male vs. female grief after, 6
   probable effects on children of, 67–68
   public acceptance of, 28–29
   statistics on, 28
   stress rating of, 29
   See also Marital stress
Divorce bereavement, symptoms of, 29–41

Index

anger/frustration, 30, 33–34
anxiety/fear, 30–32, 41–42
  in children, 46–49
  guilt, 30, 39–41
  insecurity, 30, 34–35
  listed, 30–31
  loneliness, 23, 30, 35–39, 42–43
  longing, 30, 41
  sadness/regret, 30, 32–33
Dumas, Alexander, 75

Family counselors, 76
Family service agencies, 22, 76
Fear
  of loneliness, 35
  questionnaire on, 41–42
  as symptom of divorce, 30–32
Feeling of abandonment, 3
Financial problems, 61–63
  male vs. female attitudes toward, 6
  and marital stability, 72–73
  of widows, 14–19
Food stamps, 18
Friends
  in coping with depression, 20–21
  in coping with loneliness, 36–37, 80
  Gallup Poll on typical number of, 79
Frustration as symptom of divorce, 30, 33–34
Funerals, 6, 11

Gallup surveys
  on marriage vs. single life, 81
  on typical number of friends, 79
Gibran, Kahlil, 64
Goldberg, Philip, 76
Grief, 2–7
  chronological path of, 3–4
  duration of, 4, 18–19
  in men vs. women, 4–6
  physical aspects of, 4–5
  symptoms of, in children, 47–48
  as vital process, 20

widow's, 18–19
See also Depression
Guilt, 3
  in depression, 20
  in men vs. women, 5–6
  as symptom of divorce, 30, 39–41

Health and Human Services Department, U.S., 63
Home
  ownership of, 62–63
  widow's decisions on, 14–16, 18
Human Rights Advocacy Commission, 63
Hypochondria, 3

Identification with lost partner, 3
Identity, social, 69
Income, 58–59
  and home ownership, 62–63
  and marital stress, 72–73
  pooling of, with living partner, 22
  widow's, 17–18
Insecurity as symptom of divorce, 30, 34–35
Insurance, 15
Investments, widows', 14–15
Irritability in depression, 20

Joint home ownership, 62–63

Kübler-Ross, Elisabeth, 41

Lawyers, widows' need of, 14
Life events, stressful, 29
Loneliness
  coping with, 35–39, 80–81
  depression and, 19, 23, 79
  fear of, 35
  questionnaire on, 42–43
  single life and, 79–82
  as symptom of divorce, 23, 30, 35–39
  in widowhood, 19, 23
Longing, 3
  as symptom of divorce, 30, 41

Index

Loss, pain of, see Grief
Loss of self, feelings of, 3
Lynch, James J., 79

Marital stress, 68–76
 communication problems and, 73–75
 counseling and, 75–76
 midlife crises and, 68–70
 money and, 72–73
 sex and, 70–73
Marriage
 frequency of, in U.S., 84
 See also Marital stress; Remarriage
Marriage counseling, 75–76
Marwin, Lee, 84
Masturbation, 71
Medicaid, 17
Medicare, 17
Men
 grief in, 5–6
 midlife climacteric of, 69
 sex drive of, 71–72
 as widowers, 23–24
 vs. women, in work force, 58
Menopause
 depression associated with, 69
 self-actualization after, 60
Mental health clinics, 22
Midlife climacteric, male, 68
Money
 and marital stress, 72–73
 See also Financial problems; Income
Moody, Raymond A., 41
Mourning, see Grief
Much Ado About Nothing (Shakespeare), 2

Old Age Assistance Act, 17
Orgasm, 71

Parents Without Partners, 36–37
Physical activity
 changes in, in depression, 20
 in coping with depression, 21, 80–81
Physical aspects of grief, 4–5
Pining, 3
Professional help
 for depression, 22
 See also Counseling

Questionnaires
 fear, 41–42
 loneliness, 42–43

Rahe, R. H., 28
Real estate, widowhood and, 15–16
Realization of loss, 3
Regret as symptom of divorce, 30, 32–33
Rejection, fear of, 20
Religion
 in coping with depression, 22–23
 and marriage vows, 28
 and view of death, 7
 See also Church
Remarriage
 men vs. women and, 6
 of widows and widowers, 23
 See also Stepparenting
Restlessness, 3
Routine, changing, in coping with depression, 21

Sadness as symptom of divorce, 30, 32–33
School, returning to, 59–60
 in coping with depression, 22
Self, feelings of loss of, 3
Self-control, grief and, 3, 5
Self-esteem in depression, 20
Self-image, enhancing, in coping with depression, 21
Separation, marital
 incidence of, 28
 stress rating of, 29
Sex
 missed more by men than by women, 6

95

Index

marital stress and, 70–73
widowhood and, 13
Sex drive, men's vs. women's, 69, 71–72
Shakespeare, William, 2
Single life, 78–84
  advantages of, listed, 82–83
  disadvantages of, listed, 78–79
  loneliness and depression and, 79–82
Single-parent families, 46
Social services, listed, 24–25
Stepparenting, 51–55
Stocks and bonds, widows and, 14–15
Stress
  life events rated for, 29
  marital, see Marital stress
  reducing child's, in divorce bereavement, 49–51
  of widowhood, 19–23
Suicidal feelings
  in depression, 20
  and professional help, 22

United Fund, 18, 29
Urban Institute, 83

Vocation, bereaved women and, 58–61

Weight gain and sexual problems in marriage, 72
Widowers, 23–24
Widowhood, 10–25
  financial pitfalls in, 14–19
  principle stresses of, 19–23
  sex and, 13
  social services of possible value in, listed, 24–25
  social trials in, 12–13
  society's support in, 10–11
  statistics on, 10
Women
  grief in, 5–6
  sex and, 13, 71–72
  and work, 22, 58–61
  See also Widowhood
Women's movement, 69–70
Work, bereaved women and, 22, 58–61
Work force, men vs. women in, 58

"Yours, Mine, Ours" (booklet), 55

About the Author

W. Keith Hafer has been associated with family service agencies since 1953, when he cofounded the Family Service Association of Bucks County, Pennsylvania, and served as its first president. He also was a director of the Bucks County Mental Health Society and the Tri-Counties Mental Health Clinics, Norristown State Hospital, Pennsylvania.

From 1959 to 1964, Dr. Hafer was a director of Family Service of Santa Monica, California, and from 1965 to 1970 was a member of the board of trustees of Family Service of Greater Boston, Massachusetts. Subsequently, he served for two years as a marriage and family counselor with Family Service of Norfolk, Virginia.

A former member of the faculties of the universities of Puerto Rico, Virginia, Georgia, and Texas, Dr. Hafer teaches at the University of Tampa, and with his wife is engaged in the private practice of marriage and family counseling in St. Petersburg, Florida.